AN AUTHENTIC HUMAN'S
MEANINGFUL WORK

An Authentic Human's Guide to Finding Meaningful Work

Published by Smarty Pants Press

www.authenticmeaningfulwork.com

ISBN-13: 978-0-578-75784-1

To my family, thank you for always making me laugh

ACKNOWLEDGMENTS

To the people who let me include their stories in this book, I am inspired by you every day.

To all the folks who listened to me endlessly blab on about this book and the topic, thank you.

I hope if you ever write a book, you are lucky enough to be surrounded by people like these:

Editor: Rebecca Pillsbury (duendepressbooks.com)
As you predicted, I am transformed.

Design: Antonio Garcia Martin (thisisagm.com)
You brought my words to life.

Author photo: Izabela Mattson (izabelamattson.com)
Took joyous photos

Copy editor: Kristin Thiel (kristinthiel.com)
Made what I wrote much, much better

Publishing support: Bryan Tomasovich (thepublishingworld.org)
Showed me the map through the maze

TABLE OF CONTENTS

INTRODUCTION

WHAT IS MEANINGFUL WORK?

It's hard to find work you love; it must be, if so few do. So, don't underestimate this task. And don't feel bad if you haven't succeeded yet. In fact, if you admit to yourself that you're discontented, you're a step ahead of most people.

—**Paul Graham**, "How to Do What You Love"[1]

When I was thinking about writing this book, I knew I wanted to write about more than just searching for work; there are lots of resources for that (see the appendix). But how do we find *meaningful work*? That is, work that fuels us—work that helps us grow and build community, that nourishes our sense of self-worth, where we can be our best selves. Not just our profession but the way we spend our limited time and creativity to earn a living.

Most of us will spend more time at work than we will with our loved ones. Meaningful work, whatever our definition, is critical to our well-being. The more we do what we love, the fewer headaches, crushed spirits, and world-weariness we'll experience.

In the satisfying work that I finally found for myself, I have the privilege of interacting regularly with people in their teens, twenties, and thirties, those of you called millennials and Gen Z. You all have taught me so much; I am grateful to know you.

There are so many things I appreciate and respect about millennials and Gen Z. One is your desire to be authentic, which is accompanied by a talent for quickly spotting a phony. In addition, you have an expectation of workplace diversity and inclusion that is significantly more accepting than that of previous generations. You understand that we are all better off when we accept ourselves and others, regardless of gender, economic status, race, creed, etc.

But when I talked with some of you about your work journey, I heard

> *"...with self-awareness, experimentation, persistence, and luck...I could change the course of my career in wonderful and unexpected ways."*

frustration, disappointment, confusion, and sadness. My goal with this book is to offer relief, optimism, fortitude, clarity, and hopefully even a little joy.

I learned throughout my career that there wasn't much support for finding meaningful work. There were lots of people willing to give me advice on their way, but not many people encouraged me to do it my way. I wanted to find work that matched who I was, that honored my skills—and my need to earn a living. Through my career's twists and turns, I eventually found work that was meaningful to me.

I was most successful when I was clear about myself and what I needed and wanted and when I reached out for help. I learned that with self-awareness, experimentation, persistence, and luck (for example, meeting the right person at the right time), I could change the course of my career in wonderful and unexpected ways. The road to meaningful work will be different for each person.

Each of us can make our own rules and find our own answers through using tools like the ones in this book and then running our own experiments. A career is a journey—there is no getting around that. And it's often bumpy and messy. Like many worthwhile things in life, it takes time, patience, and commitment. But I hope the ideas in this book will help ease your journey. Please take what you like and leave the rest.

Building a Foundation

This book is built around the following equation:

My values (who I am at this point in my life)
+
My skills (current and those I hope to gain)
+
My available resources (people/tools)
+
My actions (experimenting, questioning, taking risks)
=
A path to meaningful work

Part 1 of this book focuses on the first part of the formula:

understanding who you are today. It involves inner work—assessing who you are and where you're at right now. You will have different needs throughout your life; partnering, children, promotions, responsibilities, etc., will all shift your priorities. The future will be filled with surprises, so trying to figure out who you're going to be or what you'll need in your career in ten or twenty years is counterproductive. Instead, the first part of the formula is designed to help you understand who you are right now.

1. What are my values? Who am I at this point in my life?

Understanding yourself includes understanding your values. Without this self-knowledge, the chances of finding a good fit at work are hobbled. Values tend to shift slowly. We bring with us values from family, religion, hometown, ethnicity, race, education, and experience...in other words, from our roots. Values are personal; what is important to you may be different from what is important even to someone close to you. Understanding some of your key points of connection to the world (your values!) gives you a leg up in your search for meaningful work.

2. What are my skills currently, and which ones do I hope to gain?

A skills assessment starts with determining what you are naturally good at. Some of us are good with numbers, some are artistic, some pick up foreign languages easily. Acknowledging your talents is an appropriate way to begin assessing our current skill set.

The next step is to identify skills you want to learn, either because they interest you or because you know they are something useful to the career you seek. If you want to run a company, you will need managerial skills. It's possible that managerial skills training will be offered to you along the way, but are you willing to leave that to chance? I suggest you don't. It's better if you identify the skills you want to learn and find a way to gain the experience you need.

Once you understand who you are and where you are today, the next step is to understand your available choices and learn how to recognize that you have more choices than perhaps you thought. Part 2 of this book helps you identify the outer work you need to do: identifying and connecting the ideas, actions, resources, and people to help you on your journey.

3. What are my available resources?

This means identifying and activating people who can help you find meaningful work. Your community, families, friends, coworkers, neighbors, and especially those few who recognize and accept you for what you are: precious. But each of these people will play a unique role in your career search. Identifying resources means understanding which question to ask your best friend versus that contact who works in a field you're interested in. Activating means doing the work to earn others' help. You can't expect everyone to drop what's important to them to help you. You need to learn to give to get. Mentors are valuable resources, but you need to take initiative to earn their trust.

4. What actions can I take right now?

Reasonable (to you) risk-taking becomes vital to the journey of finding meaningful work. One of my favorite sayings is "Don't try harder—try different." That makes sense in principle, but what does "different" mean, if you don't know what to do? It may feel especially tough to live this idea of different when we have responsibilities. For example, trying to change the way your boss communicates is tough. If you pay attention to the way they like to communicate and work within that, your relationship may improve. Those are the kinds of tweaks of perspective I mean when I say trying different can help.

The ideas in this book helped me find meaningful work, and I trust that some of them will help you realize your options too. Experimenting with different tools and trying them out, first in low-risk situations, to understand how they fit, is an important part of the journey. These experiments are like trying on new clothes. Some look and feel great; some are terrible. We only know when we try them on.

A Path to Meaningful Work

Lewis Carroll, the author of *Alice in Wonderland*, said, "If you don't know where you're going, any road will take you there." I encourage you throughout this book to know yourself, understand what you want from a workplace (one workplace at a time), and be clear about what you want to learn when you take the next job. The You Work It sections of this book include exercises that help you clarify your values, what you want to learn, and how you might experiment in ways that you may not have considered. Your path to meaningful work will become clearer. You will find and catch the thread of what you love to do.

What I Hope You Will Gain from This Book

This isn't an "advice" book; it's a "huh, I never thought of it that way" book. In my years as a teacher, mentor, and coach, I found people benefit most from being asked thought-provoking questions. So, I hope these *ideas*—not rules—will fuel your journey. I hope you find new choices to help you navigate the world of finding work that is meaningful to you. I hope you take inspiration from some of the lessons I've learned along the way and from the stories of people (found in the case studies) who have inspired me. And then I hope you plunge forward. No one else can tell you what job to take or how to plan your career. You will know what to do. Trust yourself.

For me, meaningful work wasn't about *what* I would be when I grew up but, rather, *who* I would be. Current research[2] suggests that seeking your purpose is better than following your passion. I can be passionate about singing but know that it is not my purpose, that is, how I imagine myself contributing to the world. Passion and purpose may overlap, but for many people, they don't. One thing is certain: earning a living from having a purpose is a key to finding meaningful work. It's useful to think about what matters to you—your skills, your values, your financial needs, and other aspects of your unique experiences. Your path may lean traditional or unorthodox. It may include higher education or limited classroom education...either way, there is a path out there for you.

It's likely that some combination of passion, purpose, skills, self-compassion, hard work, and a little luck will be the hallmarks of your successful work journey—one that is driven by you and your vision and needs. As you read this book, I hope you will come to recognize in yourself what I finally came to know in myself—that we have the power to change not only ourselves but our choices. We don't have to let other people define who we are or what we can do. I believe, with my whole heart, that each of us has tremendous potential.

The uncertainty from trial and error that is involved in any change is to be expected. After all, you are trying to answer big questions: "How can I think differently about where I work, how I work, the money I make, and the life I shape that has work as a component, not as a foundation?" To that end, I recommend you start anywhere in the book that seems interesting. The road to finding enjoyable work can be full of prickly bushes and many forks. It takes an adventurous spirit and some risk-taking to make progress. But what is the alternative? Work in jobs, year in and year out, that you hate?

Whether it's via boss shopping, understanding your personal

values as they relate to work, or crafting a work schedule that "fits" with your life, I hope you will assert yourself to find work that sustains you...financially, personally, and emotionally.

I have a deep-seated belief that each of us is special, just as we are, and that once we recognize ourselves as such, doors open for us that we never thought possible. I hope you will find strength and encouragement throughout these pages to be who you are. Since you picked up this book, I can already sense that expressing your authentic self is important to you. I may not know you, but if I met you, I know I would say: *You are amazing.*

Furthermore, you can find meaningful work.

Times Are Changing, Dramatically

I am finishing the writing and editing of this book in the summer of 2020. Much of the world is under lockdown to prevent the spread of COVID-19. Unemployment is soaring, and the world economy is in a transition bordering on crisis. The ways we coped, found work, made money, and many other things could be changed forever. Today, there is no way to be sure what is going to change and how much. However, it occurs to me that the information in this book might be even more useful than before as we navigate these new waters. Once the dust settles, a postcrisis period allows us a reset button. We don't have to go back to the way things were. We probably won't have the option to go back. Instead, we can focus on where we *really* want to go.

Tip: It may be useful to keep a notebook for working through the exercises in this book. Many thoughts and ideas will come up as you read through these chapters, and it may be beneficial to have them all in one place. You can also use a computer or your phone or record by voice, but if you're able to write by hand, I recommend that. Writing by hand helps to unlock thoughts and creativity—and a notebook isn't connected to the distractions of email, text, and social media.

PART I: INNER WORK

We begin by taking a close look at ourselves. You may have done some of this work before. If so, you'll have a head start. The idea is to use your self-knowledge as home base. From there, we each fly in a different direction, but seeing ourselves as we are gives us the freedom to go to places we might never have gone. It is important that we each bring a hearty dose of self-compassion to this part of the work. I am my harshest critic. I would never judge someone else as jarringly as a do myself. I had to learn to be as gentle with myself as I was with the people I love. For me, this was part of the journey. Please know there are no right or wrong answers; there's no one to judge you. You can't make a mistake when looking into your heart. You know these answers; the exercises are here to help you name them and use them.

Now, gently, begin. Knowing yourself is vital to finding meaningful work.

CHAPTER 1

GOOD INTENTIONS, BAD ADVICE

When you're young, you're given the impression that you'll get enough information to make each choice before you need to make it. But this is certainly not so with work. When you're deciding what to do, you have to operate on ridiculously incomplete information.

—**Paul Graham**, "How to Do What You Love"

I wish I could say I have never heard someone tell a high school student:

- You must go to college.
- You must know what you want to study, before you go.
- Whatever you pick to study in college, it will change your life forever, so you better be sure.
- Wherever you choose to go to college, it will affect the rest of your life. So, you better make good grades in high school and then good grades in college. Otherwise, you are going to be a failure.
- High school is the best time of your life, so appreciate it.

You could probably add other "good" advice to this list. Counselors, parents, friends...they all mean well, but they don't necessarily know you and your dreams. They are giving "standard" advice that's been given to high school kids for generations. I have experienced my own frustration with people telling me what I can't do:

- You can't work part-time and be a manager.
- You can't negotiate to set your own work hours.
- There's no way that you can have a career working part-time.

I could go on and on, but the point is that even forty years ago, when

I was starting out, I got a lot of bad advice. It was given with good intentions. Fortunately, I ignored those people and their advice. For millennials and Gen Z, this type of advice is not only unhelpful...it's bullsh*t. I understand that this advice served people in the past, but so many things have changed in even the past twenty years that this advice is now flat-out wrong.

My suggestion for dealing with that "advice" is to listen and smile politely. Ask questions for clarification. Don't argue with the person. In the future, they might be of help to you; there is no reason to alienate them if you can avoid it. If the person is paying the bills for you (for example, if this person is part of your family), that's another issue. You may need to do at least some of what they request—or try to figure out a compromise. Nothing about this is simple or easy, but I encourage you to follow yourself, no one else, as much as you can.

What's Changed?

People give bad advice because it's what they know or what makes them feel comfortable. They may be afraid of change, and if you change, they might also have to change. They are unaware of the realities you face; they are using their experience to judge your current circumstances. Here are some of the realities that have changed since generations before millennials and Gen Z started working.[3]

- ✤ *Who we work for has changed dramatically.* In 1985, the biggest companies in the US were mostly in autos and oil. Today, they are aggregators (Amazon) and tech companies. The shift from products to services profoundly affects the work we do.

  Biggest US Companies in 1985[4]
  1. IBM
  2. Exxon
  3. General Electric
  4. AT&T
  5. General Motors

  US Biggest Companies in 2020[5]
  1. Microsoft
  2. Apple
  3. Amazon
  4. Alphabet (Google parent company)
  5. Facebook

- *Values have shifted.* Baby boomers, the generation born 1946–1964, focused on making money, having financial stability, and working hard. I have heard boomer bosses complain about the work ethic of younger generations. I try to explain that the reason for the difference isn't laziness—it's life focus. Boomers felt we needed to sacrifice family life for the security of a job. The younger people I've met are committed to a work-and-leisure balance, to making sure that your work time is spent fruitfully. I leave Gen X out of this work because I don't see the world through their eyes. I'm a boomer who has spent many years talking with, teaching, and interacting with millenials and Gen Zers.
- *The cost of college has skyrocketed.* Cost of college from 1980 to 2014 has grown at twice the rate of other consumer products (260 percent increase for college versus 120 percent for other things).[6] Student debt was $1.4 trillion in 2019.[7] With many graduates starting out with low earning potential, the ability to pay back this debt is crushing.
- *The effectiveness of a college education is in question.* The way a college education is delivered (sitting in classrooms) is questionable. As colleges are slow to update their educational methods, millennials and Gen Z have become frustrated. If the usefulness and methods of delivering knowledge had kept pace with the needs of students (and employers), the costs might be worth it. But the combination of increasing expense and reduced efficacy have made college problematic for many.
- *Technology and access to information change our daily lives.* We all have powerful computers in our pockets (cell phones), and that provides us with instant access to much of the world's knowledge. There's an app for nearly everything we want to accomplish. Thirty years ago, we got information from television, books, and newspapers.
- *Millennials have demonstrated not only a desire for balance but a demand for work that means something.* Many young people are unhappy in their current job, like they are just pushing paper around. The desire to do work that is meaningful is a driving force that many employers don't understand or know how to satisfy. This difference in values limits the jobs that millennials and Gen Z want.
- *Millennials are the largest generation in the US labor force.* In 2017, 56 million millennials (35 percent of the total workforce)[8] were working or looking for work. In that same year, 41 million boomers were in the workforce.

💎 *Progress has been made in terms of the acceptance of gender diversity in the workplace, but there's not enough equity for millennials and Gen Z.* While the business benefits of diversity and equality have been well-documented for a while now,[9] certain industries and geographies have been slower to adapt. Previously, the emphasis of diversity in the workplace highlighted women, not LGBTQIA+. I sense a hunger for a broader definition and acceptance of diversity, and those organizations that make progress in this area will benefit from millennial and Gen Z support.

What Does All This Mean for You?

Technological, financial, demographic, and social changes are leading millennials and Gen Z to think differently about work. "Infrastructure" (education, types of jobs, management, financing options, and work/life choices) has not kept up with the needs of this large and diverse group of workers. These changes clash with traditional workplace norms. Finding a company culture that matches with younger generations' values, needs, and desires is difficult.

In addition, the growth of the entrepreneurial culture has lured millennials and Gen Z to the start-up world. The gig economy (a free-market system in which organizations contract with independent workers for short-term engagements, often with no benefits) is booming. Think of jobs like driving for Uber or Lyft, renting spaces on AirBnB, or delivering for Postmates. Each of these gigs has "make your own hours" flexibility that no office job can offer. As of 2019, 57 million US workers (35 percent) are freelancers.[10]

Why This Matters to Me

I'm a baby boomer, so you might be wondering why this topic is so important to me and why I think I have something to say about it. I'll go deeper into the answer later, but for now, here's a snapshot of my journey and what led me to write this book.

I have been afforded many privileges; I identify as white and heterosexual. My race has afforded me opportunities not open to other races. Being female in a man's world, however, meant that I would be discriminated against nearly all my career.

Prior to 1980, the workplace was driven by men. They were hired, given opportunities to grow (and make mistakes), and promoted. It may be hard to imagine now, but women weren't part of management.

Most women didn't go to college. In the workplace, they were support personnel. Women were encouraged to be teachers, nurses, and bookkeepers.

When I started managing people, I was one of only two female managers in my division of more than nine hundred people. Sexism floated close to the surface but was downplayed by policies that stated it would not be tolerated. There wasn't even a mention of non-gender-conforming people. If they were hired, people who didn't "conform" were barely tolerated. And they certainly weren't given opportunities. I used these roadblocks to find a way to be myself and find innovative solutions to what I wanted for my life. The journey, the tools I used, and the risks I took are shared in this book.

Finding meaningful work seemed like the only logical path. I didn't have to do work I hated or work where I felt that I wasn't seen or appreciated. That's my definition of meaningful. Here is a snapshot of a few of the roles I've held along the way:

- *Teacher*—I worked as a secondary-school foreign language teacher. I also taught marketing and market research for over fifteen years at the college undergraduate and graduate levels, both online and face-to-face. Teaching is the foundation of my person; it's the through line of all the meaningful work experiences I've had in my life. Students almost always teach me more about being human, learning, and having determination than I teach them. This is my place.
- *Mentor*—Volunteering as a mentor to young entrepreneurs is one of my passions. For over twenty years, I have worked with both academic and community-based individuals to help them grow their ideas into companies that thrive. This work involves listening, coaching, and instilling confidence and support in learning the lesson that failure is essential to growing a successful business.
- *Digital marketer*—I love being on the leading edge of technology as it applies to business. Over my forty-year career, I've found technology advancements essential for changing the way businesses provide value to customers. Slow-to-adopt companies fade; companies with visionary leaders thrive.
- *New-media business leader*—I have been involved with millennials and Gen Z for over a decade as mother of YouTuber Jenna Marbles. I manage the legal and financial sides of her company. I understand firsthand the impact that she has on her audience. As of 2020, she has over 20 million subscribers, and her

worldwide audience watches an average of 40,000 hours of her videos a month.[11]

From teaching and mentoring to working with young people in new media, I've always been invested in the next generations. Having trained and worked as a teacher and being a technology "appreciator," I am a student of the human experience, particularly as the individual adapts to cultural and technological changes. I learned to be myself, take risks, make mistakes, and forgive myself when I made them (while I tried not to repeat them). I hope you will understand why I care about you and your journey.

Understanding Your Authentic Self

As we interact with different people, we wear different masks. We don't behave the same with our grandparents as we do with our friends. We are respectful with elders and goofy with our buddies. The problem arises when we get to the workplace and generational expectations affect our daily lives, careers, money, self-acceptance, etc. For many of us, our career journey takes up most of our time, especially in our twenties and thirties, so "faking" or hiding who we are for so long can become problematic.

Each of us brings something powerful to the world. So, our main job is to believe in and belong to ourselves.[12] This is a tall order, as we have been brainwashed into thinking that if we don't become the standard version of whatever some authority envisions us to be, then we are "less than." If we can block their opinion of us, we can find our way to our authentic selves, particularly as we find our way in the world of work.

As authentic humans searching for meaningful work, we need to recognize and appreciate ourselves exactly as we are. Of course, we still need to change, learn, and improve, but we reconcile ourselves to the fact that we are whole, special, and have something important to give to the world.

Every human being embodies dignity. Each has awe-inspiring traits— bodies, souls, spirits, and senses. The glory of being able to move and sing and laugh! We can taste ice cream and love a child.

Strength and power come from self-acceptance and ego-less self-appreciation and compassion. Confidence is derived from an honest understanding of our strengths and weaknesses and a willingness to continuously learn and grow.

Maybe you're thinking, *all that sounds great, but I don't feel confident when I am staring into the face of a boss or someone else who judges me harshly.* Here's my truth: even today, I sometimes feel self-conscious, confined, lost, confused, and like a phony. The rest of the time, this is my self-talk:

- ❧ I'm good.
- ❧ I can do this.
- ❧ I deserve all that is good.
- ❧ I know how to be in the world.

My goal is to make my actions and feelings congruous. That is, I am the same person no matter where I am. I am respectful to my elders and goofy with my friends at home, but when I'm at work, I am that same person. I don't hide who I am. I don't pretend to be smarter or dumber. I humbly offer my talents to the organization, contribute, and learn. I don't let someone else's thoughts about me affect my behavior. What they think of me isn't my business. Sure, my contribution certainly is the business of my employer. But my employer and coworkers don't get to define me and my work. If you are able to hold yourself in the esteem you deserve, or if you are working on doing that, you are on the right road.

For today, when you have moments of doubt, will you please accept that, to me, you are unique and important? I've never met you, but I know if I did, I would recognize how uniquely wonderful you are. How precious you are. I hope you agree that there's no one else like you in the world.

Finding meaningful work is about knowing who we are, what we value, and what we have to offer. Finding and accepting our authentic selves is the beating heart of the journey to meaningful work. My desire is to support you on this journey by offering not advice but tools to help you find work that satisfies your financial and emotional well-being.

Make a list of your unique qualities.

You may be wondering: *How do I know what makes me unique?*

Think about what your friends, family, teachers, coworkers, etc., say about you. Consider yourself from their perspective.

Think about people you admire. What unique qualities do they possess?

When you review their list and compare it to yours, you'll find you have more in common than you think.

Make sure there are at least ten things on your list. Some will be specific just to you. It's OK if some are qualities that all humans have, like senses. The ability to smell and to taste—these are not ordinary but powerful. I hope we learn to appreciate them, not take them for granted.

Think about what you love, no judgments. What do you love so much that when you do it, time means nothing? Maybe it's appreciating music or coloring. We're not looking necessarily for big things—we're looking for the things that make you, you.

CHAPTER 2

CHANGING A LIFETIME OF "UNBELONGING" MESSAGES

I n the previous chapter, we discussed how well-meaning but bad advice hurts us in many ways. We can't always stop people from sharing their opinions, but we can choose whether we let that advice in or whether we kick it to the curb. I call this Velcro® or Teflon™. If the advice lifts you up, it may be worth paying some attention to—get out the Velcro®. If the advice brings you down or makes you feel "less than," then bring out the Teflon™. Let it slide right off.

The difficulty in accepting ourselves as we are is that we have been "programmed" by our families, our schools, our places of worship, our culture, etc., to think of ourselves in a certain way. *I am not pretty, or I am too pretty. I have this body type or that one. I have a "wrong" way of perceiving the world.* All these are definitions others place upon us. They do that so they can be comfortable with their world. If they can put us into a category, they can go on about their day without any fuss. When we challenge their view, they feel attacked, small, and vulnerable. They'd rather put the pressure on us than experience those feelings. The more forceful their response, the more threatened they likely feel. We can't change them, but we can work on our attitude toward what they say and do to us.

Conditioning Starts Early

From an early age, we are asked questions about our future. We are given messages about success, our potential, our role in the family and society that may do more harm than good. Messages can be subtle, or they can be rammed down our throats. These can hinder our ability to find meaningful work as an adult.

Here's an example of a conversation between a teacher or parent and a middle schooler.

Adult: What do you want to be when you grow up?
Kid: I don't know.
Adult: You don't, huh? Well, you must have some ideas. Look at all the successful people around you. They probably knew what they wanted to do from a young age. They concentrated on getting good grades, thinking about the right college. They made something of themselves.
Kid: Um...

This conversation changes slightly but is basically the same in high school.

Adult: What are you going to study in college? Where are you going to work when you graduate?
Young adult/Teen: I'm not sure I'm going to college. I don't know.
Adult: What? What do mean? You have to go to college. You won't be able to get a good job without going to college. Your first job out of high school is really important. You can't just work at the Pizza Shop!
Young adult/Teen: I'm trying to figure all that out.

In college or when a young adult is first working, the conversation becomes even more problematic.

Adult: How's college/your job?
Young adult: Good.
Adult: What's your plan?
Young adult: My plan?
Adult: Yeah, what are you going to do next?

This conversation may then veer off into discussion about the young adult's:

❧ Potential
❧ Expectations
❧ Money

Young adult: I wish I knew. The closer I get to graduation/the longer I work at this job, the worse I feel and the harder it is.
Adult: Well, you better get your act together.

How You Could React to This Question

Here's an example of a real conversation I overheard between another adult and my twenty-year-old daughter:

Random adult: What are your goals? Where do you see yourself in five years?
Jenna: How should I know? I'm a kid.

These questions and the pressure they apply is one way that adults push us into doing what they want. The brainwashing starts early. We help ourselves if we learn to manage the pressure and/or find an answer that makes the person and their questions go away, without being rude. Here are a couple other sample answers to either try out or laugh at. Your choice.

Adult: What's your plan?
You: I'm glad you asked. I have several ideas. I'd like to share them with you when I have more clarity.
(Or, taking a humorous approach): I'm thinking of joining the circus. I have real potential as a clown.

Adults tend to like kids who follow their rules, in work, relationships, religion, and politics. We may notice the approval and positive feedback they get. For the rest of us, the questions act like a hammer, banging away at our self-esteem.

This battering drives us to believe we have to conform. But conforming is the enemy of creativity. It takes skill to walk the line between what others want for us and what we want for ourselves. It also takes deprogramming and courage.

Myths of Being a Grown-Up Working Human

In addition to pressure, some adults like to throw around conventional wisdom. I call them myths. The advice might be conventional, but I'm not sure it's wisdom. Pay attention when you begin to notice variations on these themes. Statements like these are traps: "You seem like such a smart person. Why can't you decide on one thing and stick to it?" Be ready with a self-affirming but not dismissive response. Listen to what is being offered and decide whether to employ Velcro® or Teflon™.

Myth 1—People should know what they want to do.

Some people who look like they know what they are doing, do, in fact, know. But lots of us are faking it. I usually go that route. It's easier for me to act confident and fumble along than to admit I'm lost and ask for help.

I have learned that most people who seem like they have it all together are often bluffing. Acting like we know what we're doing isn't a bad thing. It can be a strategy for success. But it can also be a trap. Once you act as if you're confident in your path, other people begin to have expectations of you. And those expectations can become a burden.

Myth 2—Checking off boxes is a good way to find meaningful work.

A box-checker is someone who uses an existing framework (for example, college, job, marriage, kids) as a template for their life. There is nothing wrong this. I'm a box-checker. I like when things go according to plan. But when I didn't know what to do with my life, I didn't fumble around; I looked for another box—I did what a lot of other people did. I tried college. I went to a two-year college then finished at a four-year college. It took me seven years, but I did it.

College seemed like a place to land that would give me a safe harbor while I figured out how to earn a living. I had worked several boring, low-paying jobs that I was 100 percent sure I didn't want to do for the rest of my life. These jobs were the best possible motivator for me to go to college.

Don't be limited by box-checking. It may be useful for finding meaningful work, but there are many paths outside of these standard boxes. Some involve college; some don't. Today, a more common path than in the past is entrepreneurial, and it has different facets:

- ✤ Work for a start-up.
- ✤ Work for a small company or nonprofit (these start-ups can be useful for broadening our skills base because we often get to wear multiple hats).
- ✤ Pursue something on the side. I read a story about a premed student who pushed the first year of medical school off in order to try out to be the mascot of a college football team! (Imagine that conversation with the parents.)

The path is different for everyone. Just because you don't automatically realize a way forward doesn't mean there isn't a way. There is a way—you have to work to find it. Acknowledge your uniqueness. Be brave. You can do this.

Myth 3—Following a recommended plan will solve all your career or money problems.

Life happens. Things change, people get sick, money disappears, support evaporates. A good plan is great, but that plan better be flexible. Solving problems is the life of a grown-up.

For example, if you are not contributing to or earning your own living, then the keeper of the purse strings will influence, in significant ways, the way your plan goes. I am advocating for being careful about the outside resources you accept and the terms for that acceptance. Free rides have a way of not being free.

My remedy was to have my own money, that I earned and saved, so I could do what I wanted. I saw what happened to people when they lived on someone else's nickel. I didn't like those obligations. With my own income, I was free to make decisions about my future.

Money is only one trap. When I study or take a job that someone else wants me to, I may find that it causes more problems than it solves. Try things but understand your motives for doing so.

Myth 4—Don't complicate your life with too many choices; keep it simple.

Adults made everything seem straightforward. Go to college. Get a job. Get married. If I could just think in these black-and-white extremes—this is good, and this is bad; this comes first, and that comes second—I'd be OK. But then I grew up and realized that, in fact, there are many possible paths to meaningful work and a happy life. In fact, life isn't so simple.

The biggest problem was that I was unaware that I had been brainwashed into thinking the way they wanted me to. I didn't hear my own self-talk. If I did what they wanted, I felt accepted. If I didn't, I felt worthless. I either did a great job on everything or if I failed at one thing, nothing else I did was right. I let negative voices take over. It takes self-awareness and practice to stop the hamster wheel of judgment from turning in my head.

Relying too much on family or societal norms for validation is the enemy of authenticity. It robs us of our flexibility and creativity.

It blocks us from seeing our choices. As we embrace our true selves, we begin to change the voices that tell us we're not enough. It doesn't happen overnight; it's a slow process of chipping away the armor we've built to protect our precious selves.

A Word about Discrimination

Many of us have been wounded by people who were wounded themselves. Much of the damage is deep and seemingly permanent for both parties. At its darkest

"...in your own way, stand tall for yourself. When you can and how you can. Not every day, every minute, but in whatever way you can manage."

and worst, it is entrenched in our legal system and supported by societal systems like housing, education, and employment.

It affects how we feel about ourselves, how we conduct ourselves, and how we perceive our places in the world. If you are one of those people who feels wounded, I regret to say, you are in good company. While our stories may vary, the result can be the same—and it is heartbreaking.

When we compare ourselves to others and/or buy into what we think others think about us, we take on a heavy load. It takes grit to stand tall in the face of discrimination.

You may be thinking, *Not everyone can be brave.* I hear you. I am asking that you, in your own way, stand tall for yourself. When you can and how you can. Not every day, every minute, but in whatever way you can manage.

Pay attention to the messages that are playing in your head.

Believing what others have told you about yourself that doesn't match who you are can block you from finding meaningful work. As you begin to understand your special attributes, think about the messages you received that made you discount these qualities. The perspective of families, religions, traditions, and many other sources may contribute to your negative self-image.

> *A word about forgiveness. We have a right to be angry when we are mistreated. It's important to take time to acknowledge and process our feelings. We don't have to accept the unacceptable, but we also don't have to carry open wounds with us forever.*

Begin to pay attention to the messages that are playing in your head. Notice the amount of chatter. The repetition. The way it makes you feel.

What is the main topic of the chatter? Does it vary, or is it centered on one person or one incident?

If it's one thing, try writing down what it is. Be specific. If it varies, try to capture categories of concern. Work? Relationship? Family?

Write down the categories that take the most energy. For one entire day, put a check mark next to the category every time you catch yourself thinking about something within it. If a day seems too long, try it for an hour.

This will take time and attention. The benefit to you will be awareness. We can't begin to change behavior unless we recognize it. Once you acknowledge the pattern in your thinking, you can begin to change it for the better.

Work out which of these messages are useful and which are harmful. Are you engaging in all-or-nothing thinking? Try to recognize when you are doing this. Here are some sample messages:

❧ I'll never get promoted.

- No matter what I try, it's not going to work out.
- My parents said I'd never amount to anything, and they were right.
- I should have stayed at my old job; it wasn't that bad.

Here are some things you can say to replace those messages:

- Old: I'll never get promoted. **New: I don't know what the criteria are for getting promoted; I'm going to find out.**
- Old: No matter what I try, it's not going to work out. **New: Last week I tried speaking up. I was uncomfortable, but I did it.**
- Old: My parents said I'd never amount to anything, and they were right. **New: I'm so proud of myself for trying something different.**
- Old: I should have stayed at my old job; it wasn't that bad. **New: I talked to my friend about my old job, and they reminded me how miserable I was. This job isn't perfect, but at least I'm trying something new.**

Do you see how substituting a revised message can improve the way you think about yourself? I hope so. Changing messages that are no longer useful opens up new ways of thinking about yourself and what you do with your time. Humans are fragile. We need all the help and support we can muster. You can do this. Start today.

CHAPTER 3

MY PATH TO FINDING MEANINGFUL WORK

You may be asking yourself, who is this Debbie person? In this chapter, I share a bit about my journey and the path I took to finding meaningful work. Hopefully, you will understand how my journey informed my recognition for the need to be authentic at work. I am special like you, but not more than you. You may find examples in my journey that help you understand yours, but remember that your journey remains yours and yours alone.

A key point I want to make here is that everything about my career—every job I took and every person I worked for—taught me something. What I hated about one job helped me know what to avoid in my next position. Nothing was a waste; there are no mistakes—only experiences to learn from. At the time, it might have felt like I'd made a bad decision, but in retrospect, the lesson I learned from that experience is the one I needed. I wouldn't be here today if I hadn't had each of these jobs.

My First Jobs

I grew up in Massachusetts. When I was thirteen, my mother saw an ad in the paper for a mother's helper (now called a nanny) for a one-year-old baby. The job meant that I would leave home and live with strangers for the entire summer at their house on Cape Cod.

We drove to the stranger's house, my mother spoke to them, and it was decided I would take the job. As soon as school got out, I went to live with them until school started again in September. I'll leave out the details of that experience, but I'll say that I was scared and sad, and it was hard. I learned a lot during that summer and subsequent mother's helper jobs. These experiences contributed to making me the person I am today. While it may sound strange for my mother to hand me off to strangers, remember this was a different time, when this kind of trust was common.

After I babysat summers on Cape Cod for three years, I was ready to work a regular summer job. I returned to the Cape the next summer looking for new work, and this time I would also have to find a place to live. Where did a sixteen-year-old live if not at home? A boarding house! I had a room with no meals provided, but there was a hot plate, and dishes could be washed in the sink.

During these years, over school breaks, I held the following fantastic (cough, cough) jobs:

- **Dry cleaning clerk**—I lasted a few weeks, and then I couldn't take it anymore. All those cleaning fumes! I quit.
- **Chamber maid at a motel**—This job was seven days a week, all summer. It included cleaning several rooms full of people on vacation from their regular lives. I cleaned up a lot of sand, and to this day, I leave a hotel room as nice as I can with a tip for the cleaning person.
- **Waitress**—My only restaurant experience was waitressing at this terrific seafood and burger joint. I gained fifteen pounds as I ate my way through fried clams and milkshakes.
- **Dunkin' Donuts**—Dunkin' is pre-Starbucks. Good coffee. As an aside, the summer I worked there, it was one of three jobs I held at the time (I was saving money to travel to Europe). I love donuts, but I didn't want a weight-gain repeat, so I ate only one donut the whole summer—on my last day of work.
- **Governess**—How I got this job is another whole story, but I worked at Mar-a-Lago (pre–Donald Trump), taking care of the grandchildren of Mrs. Marjorie Merriweather Post. For two weeks over Christmas 1968, I took these two wealthy children to their swimming lessons, tennis lessons, etc. I lived at Mar-a-Lago in the Blue room. I missed Christmas Eve, Christmas Day, New Year's Eve, and my birthday with my family—which was hard, but I got to live in an amazing house and witness what it's like to live like old money rich people. This lifestyle left an impression on me. I learned that money made things easier...but also harder. The kids I took care of got to see their grandmother maybe once a day for fifteen to thirty minutes. They all had to be dressed in the exact same clothes. They spent very little time with their parents. Having money, while good for having a place to live and for food, doesn't mean you have a happy life.
- **Law firm file clerk**—This was my first real grown-up job. I filed legal papers, delivered documents (this was pre-FedEx), ran errands, and took the partners' cars to the car wash. I learned a lot about legal affairs and what it was like to work in an office. I was in

the office only about 60 percent of the time, but this experience taught me that I probably was not meant to sit in an office at all. I liked the freedom of being out and about, and I did not mind getting an attorney's car washed if it meant I didn't have to sit all day and file papers!

- ⊕ **Shoe store clerk**—A big chain shoe store hired me to be a salesclerk. I wasn't a great salesperson. The management kept trying to get me to sell every woman a matching handbag when she bought shoes. My bosses were very nice and let me go as soon as Christmas was over. Interestingly, later in my career, I would come to appreciate how hard it is to be a good salesperson and that it's not about dragging someone to another part of the store to try to upsell them. It's about listening to the customer, seeing if the offering matches what they need, and then providing that to them in a way that helps them. Some pushy salespeople probably do well, but the most successful salespeople I know are quiet; they know how to listen and ask good questions. They know that a happy customer is their ticket to future sales.

- ⊕ **Kids clothing store clerk**—I loved this job. Moms and kids... it was great. Again, management wanted me to drag people over to another part of the store to show them merchandise that they hadn't asked for. I was fired from this job because I just couldn't do that to customers.

Each of these jobs taught me something; each position had benefits and problems. I learned to be independent and self-sufficient, assets I value to this day. From all these experiences, I learned that I could do different things, even if I didn't like to do them.

I learned that if I was clear about what I wanted to learn; I could be more discerning about what job I might try next instead of just job hopping.

> *"I learned that if I was clear about what I wanted to learn; I could be more discerning about what job I might try next instead of just job hopping."*

There's nothing wrong with working a lot of jobs or working only a few jobs. There is no "right" number of jobs to have. However, we can move from job to job without much thought, and we'll learn something, but we won't necessarily learn the things that will help us get to meaningful work faster. When we think about the skills we want to gain, we have a better chance of taking a job that feels like a step in the right direction. The energy spent adjusting to a new environment can teach us to be flexible, or it can waste a lot of energy that could be devoted to learning other valuable skills.

College Days

I decided to enroll in community college because I was sick of working these boring jobs. They were a terrific motivator. I loved my time at Cape Cod Community College. I was fortunate that the quality of teachers was outstanding for a two-year school, since many people loved the isolation and beauty of the area in winter. I took out loans, lived on my own, and scraped by working part-time jobs and using food stamps. As I finished my two-year degree, it seemed logical to apply to university.

Career Aspiration #1: French Teacher

I had always wanted to be a French teacher. In the 1970s, becoming a teacher was an accepted career path for women. I applied to the University of Massachusetts at Amherst and was accepted. I decided to take a year off before starting school to save money and travel. I worked three jobs to get the funds to go to Europe for four months. I saved $900, which was a fortune. I spent $200 on roundtrip airfare. The remainder allowed me to travel to France, Belgium, Luxembourg, Spain, England, and Ireland. I made this journey thinking it would improve my ability to be a good French teacher when I graduated. My eye was on the prize...a job as a teacher.

My financial aid package included work-study money, so after I started classes, I took a job at the university library. Always a big fan of books, I felt like I had the whole world at my fingertips. I remember stumbling upon Van Gogh's letters to his brother, Theo. I took that book home and read every word. I could relate to his fear and longing. My love for books and libraries grew, and I began to notice another path to earning a living doing something I loved (spoiler alert: I soon became a librarian). I was still sure about teaching, but my time at the library informed another path.

I did my student teaching at a middle school. I loved the kids, but I didn't love the school environment. In the teacher's lounge, teachers discussed kids in unkind ways. I could see myself teaching; I couldn't see myself working at a school. I was at my first career crossroads. What in the world was I going to do now? I was ready for the next step of the journey.

Career Aspiration #2: Librarian

I was twenty-five-years old. It had taken me seven years, but I was about to graduate from college. Since I had no idea what to do, I decided to stay in Amherst and continue to work full-time at the university library. It would be, I thought, an easy transition. The work wasn't hard, and I could still be around all the art and literature I wanted. But after about six months of working full-time, I still loved the library, but I was bored with the job.

Backed by all the useful skills I'd learned at the library, I got a higher-level library job with an air force contractor located in Arlington, Virginia, just a quick walk to the Pentagon. I stumbled into the job but came to really love it. I decided to go back school to get my master's degree in library science. Why?

- I loved working in the library at a level above the reshelving of books that I did at the college library.
- It was a one-year master's program.
- My employer would pay for my classes.
- I thought the program would be manageable while I had a full-time job.

Before I finished my degree, I got engaged, and with my husband-to-be (also my future-kids' dad), I moved to Rochester, New York. Over the next year, I worked at the public library there. I learned a lot about the challenges and contributions of community libraries. I continued my master's at the local public university, paying for the classes myself because I wanted to keep the momentum going.

Finally, I landed a well-paying job at Rochester's largest employer, Kodak, the photography company. My job was to run one of its corporate libraries while I finished my master's. When I joined the company, it was the thirtieth-largest corporation in the US, with 128,000 worldwide employees, 51,000 in Rochester. I had no idea that the corporate environment would teach me so much about business and myself.

If you are familiar with the television series *Mad Men*, you may have an idea of what working at Kodak in the 1980s was like. While the show is set from 1960 to 1970, the workplace depicted in it is sobering and shockingly realistic even outside that decade. In fact, I had trouble watching it because it reminded me too much of what work was like. In some ways, the workplace has changed, and, in others, it still has a ways to go. What seemed "normal" in 1980 would seem unfair today.

We have made progress. I mention this to help you understand where and how I learned what I learned and how it served me later in my career.

The job at Kodak had many positives:

- The company paid for the rest of my degree.
- I had excellent pay and benefits.
- High-quality training programs were available.

And some negatives (for me) were:

- The company was big; starting there was like moving from a small town to a major city. I felt overwhelmed in the beginning.
- When I was hired, the HR person said, "You know there's no career path for you here, right?"
- The company was white and male dominated, with few women managers and little other diversity.
- Most women were secretaries who "got ahead" by waitressing at the executive (all-male) dining room on their lunch break. These talented, intelligent women were vying for a promotion by serving their male bosses' food. It made me insane.

I was one of only a handful of women managers in my division of nearly one thousand people, and at least according to that one HR person, I had no chance of moving further up the corporate ladder. Working at a corporation with over $25 billion in sales that was nearly one hundred years old was interesting, enriching, and immensely frustrating. Because I was cocky (I was a know-it-all), I said things much more directly than the organization was used to. I didn't like, nor was I good at, the politics required to advance.

Despite my lack of understanding of how to play the "game," I was recognized as someone who could get things done. My job was a newly created position. I was establishing an information center that was part library and part information management consulting. Hundreds of internal consultants, serving Kodak units all over the world, depended upon the center to do their jobs. I had no idea what I was getting myself into, but I thrived in bringing order to the disorganization that I found.

I understood that I was good at making order out of chaos—the more challenging, the better. This position was the start of my career in unstructured jobs, jobs that no one had had before me. I learned that my ability to see how to push forward in sticky, complicated work environments was one of my biggest strengths. I was unfazed by complex projects with multiple clients and resources. After this, I had an idea that "ordinary" jobs probably wouldn't work for me.

I began to look for a different job inside Kodak. There were hundreds of jobs open, but what was I qualified for? I was determined to find interesting work, continuously learn, and get paid well.

Career Aspiration #3: Consultant

While at Kodak, I was exposed to the work of self-employed consultants. In the back of my mind, I had always wanted to have my own business, but it wasn't something that women did. Besides, I had small children. What business could I start? I watched while the males broke away from Kodak and moved into self-employed consulting. I knew that working for someone else, doing the work my boss thought was important, wasn't going to satisfy my itch for spending my precious time and energy in a way that meant something to me.

Staying at Kodak seemed to be in my best interest, for the foreseeable future. I wanted to work part-time to be home to raise my kids, and I wanted a new challenge. The training opportunities were outstanding. The question was, what did I want to learn? I asked people I trusted and considered mentors both inside and outside Kodak where they thought I needed to grow. These mentors suggested two things: finance and marketing. I wasn't 100 percent sure what these disciplines involved, but I learned why they were important to me: I would need them later to pursue my own consulting business.

To gain experience within those fields, I applied for—and landed—another newly created position: director of competitive intelligence. I was only vaguely familiar with this discipline but soon learned it was an actual career. By gathering and analyzing data on Kodak's competitors, I would help my company grow and provide more customers with competitive services and products. This job required not only research skills, which I had, but also the ability to synthesize and make recommendations based on the limited information available. I loved this job. I didn't have staff to worry about, so I could just do my job. I liked my boss and my coworkers. I felt lucky. Once again, this was a job no one had had before me; I could make it my own.

This job let me get to know a lot of different people from various sectors of the corporation. While I wasn't in finance, my boss reported to the finance director. This was my chance to learn how important understanding financials is to growing a company. Everything we did was grounded in delivering value. I also learned about market research, how to ask good questions, and the importance of understanding customer needs. My belief that most good work was grounded in teamwork was reinforced. Teams got things done that would overwhelm any one individual. Goal setting became key to measuring progress.

While at Kodak, I learned that self-knowledge, broad experiences, and good working relationships were valuable resources. Did I always make great career decisions? I don't know. I took advantage of some opportunities and missed others. I was afraid, and I was bold. In other words, I was human. Once I accepted that, I felt better about my future.

Work Gets More Meaningful

I left Kodak in 1998 to start my first business, a consulting company. It was exciting to make the leap and learn so much about business and myself. Everything was going well until September 11, 2001. The attack on the US brought the economy to its knees. Every client pulled their contracts. The business was dead. I had learned more valuable lessons. I loved working independently, I liked controlling who I worked for (my customers), and I liked building a business. I figured out I could grow an income from doing a few different things: teaching and independent consulting. I started over.

I started teaching at the graduate level in digital marketing, business communication, and market research. All the things I studied in college were great, but they didn't matter at all to my career. Having a master's degree was instrumental in getting some of the jobs I had (including teaching), but the subject of my master's didn't matter. It was just a credential to be checked off in a set of boxes. I was teaching what I had learned in the jobs that I had taken across the previous decade.

I loved teaching. Developing new courses was a lot of work, and the money wasn't great, but the students were fantastic. They challenged me, humbled me, and taught me, and I loved them for it. I taught online and face-to-face. I got a lot of practice speaking in front of people. My students showed me that if I outlined a learning path and structured class so they had maximum interaction with each other (instead of just listening to me), they would teach each other in fun and fruitful ways.

Fast-forward to 2012. A new opportunity arose to use many of the skills I had learned up this point in my career. Running a business, including managing people, financials, marketing, and legal, had prepared me to accept this wonderful opportunity.

My daughter, Jenna, asked me to help her with her business. I was thrilled and daunted. Could I do it? Would it damage my relationship with my child? Could I add enough value to her business? Jenna and I had a long discussion about roles, responsibilities, and how we'd always put our relationship first. I'm happy to report that eight years later, we continue to make it work.[13]

Not only do I get to use all my expertise and learn about new industries, technology, and customers but I get to help my child establish herself financially. I am able to be myself and be of service to one of the most important people in my life. I earn a living and have a flexible schedule that allows me to do the things that make me happy outside of work. I am trusted and respected.

This may be something any parent could do in principle, but my business training uniquely qualifies me to be a trusted manager and advisor. Our commitment to our relationship first and business second isn't easy, but it's one thing that makes this job so important to me.

New Lessons in Starting and Running a Business

Until she hired me, Jenna had run all the parts of her business by herself with minimal help. For a young content creator whose business was rapidly growing, this was a challenge. As someone with years more work experience, I brought skills and knowledge to the relationship, but I too had lessons to learn.

1. The "products" of the business—videos, etc.—were 100 percent Jenna's. I had a lot to learn about:

   - YouTube
   - Finding trusted business resources in the "entertainment" space
   - Working together with Jenna

2. Running someone else's business was a challenge at first. The important decisions were Jenna's, not mine, but I had to figure out what I could do that would help her with her money and prevent unfavorable business dealings. For example, I make sure that:

   - The money that is owed gets collected
   - Contracts and agreements are drawn up fairly and correctly and are followed

- Taxes, incorporating the business, copyright, and trademarks are dealt with
- IT (website, email, servers, etc.) is managed
- Relationships with accountants, attorneys, and licensing are handled
- Employees are respected, listened to, managed, and paid
- Problems are anticipated and prepared for

3. Every business needs to grow. In Jenna's case, she was overwhelmed with opportunities. As her channel grew, so did the requests for her to appear in films and on television, to write a book, and on and on. Brands wanted in on her explosive growth. Jenna was careful about the avenues she explored and the way she spent her time. I admire much about her, but this aspect was one of the trickiest. She could make a lot of money by doing brand deals on her channel. She chose not to do that, which was not an easy choice. My job was to help vet opportunities so Jenna could decide what was best for her.

Since 2014, I have also run the Jenna Julien podcast (youtube.com/user/JennaJulienPodcast/videos). We follow the same process as with Jenna's video channel. Jenna and Julien do all the production. With their guidance, I help manage the outsourcing of postproduction, sales, financials, legal, IT, licensing, etc.

I love working from home, but it takes discipline. I am able to get up, eat breakfast, and get to work right away. I work for four to six hours a day. One thing about working in a small business is that the business never closes. If it's 9:00 p.m. and there's something that needs to be done, it gets handled. This fits with how I work best: less structure, more autonomy, more accountability, and the ability to innovate suit me.

I acknowledge how every job I ever had has contributed to my ability to do the work I do now. I take immense pride and joy in being able to earn a living by helping one of my children learn, grow, and earn her living in a way that meets her needs for creativity and lifestyle.

Observe patterns in the jobs you've had.

Make a list of all the jobs you've had. Include gigs like babysitting, lawn mowing, and volunteer work. Don't worry about chronology (although it may help you to remember by thinking in that way). Beside each, add a note about what you learned at that gig. Don't think about it too hard—keep it simple. When you review your notes, you may notice some interesting patterns or realize some things about your journey that you hadn't noticed before.

CHAPTER 4

TAKE STOCK OF YOUR TOOL KIT

I f you did the You Work It exercise in the previous chapter, you have an initial understanding of where you've been, in terms of your job history, and some of the skills and lessons you've learned along the way. Now, let's assess where all of those experiences have led you. One way to better understand where you're at today is to assess your strengths and weaknesses—the elements in your personal job-hunting tool kit.

If you roll your eyes at the thought of listing your strengths and weaknesses, you are not alone. For me, identifying these is an ongoing, maddening exercise. I don't want to review what I'm doing well and where I'm screwing up (this is how I think of my weaknesses). But I keep assessing them anyway, because I want to maximize the amount of time I spend doing what I like and succeed at and minimize the time I spend frustrated. When I know who I am and where I want to go, the path to success is smoother and more direct.

Focusing on our strengths and understanding our weaknesses paves the way for a realistic assessment of our evolving selves. No one stays the same, or if they do, they have to invest a lot of energy in staying that way.

Life affects us. We are tested. We move, take new jobs, marry, have children, and so on. We grow more when are aware of what we do well and when we notice where we are weak.

Focus on Your Strengths, Not Your Weaknesses—More Bad Advice

A quick online search shows lots of articles that tell you to focus on your strengths and ignore your weaknesses. If this is what you choose and it works, great. For me, this is bad advice because:

- ❧ Weaknesses can be turned into strengths.
- ❧ In order to be "successful," we need to understand our shortcomings so we can learn to mitigate them.

❦ We learn more from our mistakes than our successes, so making mistakes is essential.

It's common for people in their twenties and thirties (of any generation) to bank on their strengths to get them through. Confidence is needed to start companies, lead social change, etc. There is a difference between being confidently humble enough to continue learning and expecting that others will give us a chance to lead simply because we think we deserve it. Own your strengths, but don't fall in love with them. It's not easy to be objective about ourselves, but it's some of the most productive work we'll do as we look for work that honors our authentic selves.

There is no one in the world who has my exact set of positives, shortcomings, and skills. No one else was raised in my birth order in my family, in my country, with my education. Part of understanding myself is knowing specifically where I'm strong and where I fall short.

Spending time thinking about our strengths is beneficial in a number of ways:

❦ It reduces stress.
❦ We'll be more successful, whatever that means to each of us, if we focus on a positive outcome. Imagine an Olympic swimmer standing poolside thinking only about all the things that could go wrong.
❦ Mood swings even out. This doesn't mean that everything is always great. A positive outlook isn't a view through rose-colored glasses, but it does help focus our attention on what we can do to improve a situation.
❦ Understanding ourselves, especially our strengths, helps us to focus on and demonstrate to others what we are capable of.
❦ Confidence is sexy. Self-understanding, and the poise that comes with it, serves all parts of life.

Spending time thinking about our weaknesses is also beneficial. It may make us more open to constructive criticism. At work, we will get criticism, some of it deserved, some not so much. Either way, it's part of being an adult. It's an important skill to learn to listen to feedback with an open mind. And just because someone says this is how they perceive us and our work doesn't make it true. There may be a seed of something to be aware of that will serve us. But we don't have absorb the assessment as 100 percent true.

Spending quality time with our weaknesses needs a gentle touch. I think I understand all the ways I don't measure up. In reality, unless I have asked people (like bosses and colleagues) what weaknesses they notice in me, I probably miss some things. An awareness of our shortcomings is valuable, but beating ourselves up for mistakes is not. Here are some different approaches to consider:

- We can think about "areas for improvement" rather than dwelling on "gosh, I'm a failure"; this leads to a better outcome.
- As with strengths, picking two to three weaknesses to think about and work on is best. If the list is too long, it's overwhelming. If we ignore our weaknesses completely, we lose an opportunity to feel good about our progress and to become more effective at work.
- Asking someone we trust to help us understand our shortcomings is valuable. Each of us will need to take the initiative to ask.

What's in This (So-Called) Tool Kit?

For the purposes of this book, there are two categories in each person's tool kit:

- Strengths and current skills
- Weaknesses and skill gaps

I have combined strengths and skills because these make up the "plus" side of the tool kit. Weaknesses and skill gaps are joined for this exercise because these are opportunities we have to grow and change. We can build on both. We are better served when we are clear about what we want to learn and change, rather than letting fate or our employer dictate where we spend our limited time and energy.

A **strength** is what we have a natural talent for. For instance, some people are good at connecting with people; they have an innate ability to empathize or listen without judgment and make friends easily.

A **skill** can be learned and built upon. Those who struggle to make friends or get along with coworkers can learn tools and strategies to improve their people skills. Whereas a strength might be a genuine enjoyment of people, a skill might be the learned ability to work effectively on a multidisciplinary team.

In other words, we can learn skills (for example, how to use Microsoft Office, how to play a video game, how to communicate in Spanish), but strengths are things we are born with (for example, athletic ability, an ear for music, our personality).

A **weakness** is where we are not as effective as we'd like. Maybe we are too focused on details. This might be considered a strength in some environments. But when we take a job where we need to see the big picture, being too focused on the details is a problem. Particularly if we are managing people. Details are, of course, important. But if we focus on the details and not the people, there may be unintended, negative consequences. Weaknesses are born out of our genetics and the environment we were raised in, and importantly, we all have them. Every one of us.

We may recognize our weaknesses when we have trouble saying no, lack confidence in our abilities under pressure, or neglect asking for help. When we are aware of these shortcomings, we can work to find ways to improve our abilities.

Skill gaps are competencies that we have identified we want to learn or improve on. Unless we do a clear assessment of these, we end up stumbling along.

Your employer might suggest a course and offer to pay for it. You may take advantage of that opportunity. But that is what this current employer wants you to learn. If you identify what will help you grow and lead you to the opportunities you seek, then you are taking charge. Paying attention to your weaknesses and gaps is an important step. Continuous learning is key to a meaningful work journey. Asking a current employer to give you a chance to manage a team or learn how to read a financial statement is one way to fill a skill gap. As you consider your future work journey, you will realize new, unexpected skills that will serve you.

MEANINGFUL CASE
WORK | STUDY

Where did you grow up?

I was born in New Jersey, and when I was thirteen, we moved from the inner city in New Jersey to rural Pennsylvania, so that was a quite a transition. I was a city kid in the woods, and in this town, people didn't like the city kid.

What did your parents do for a living?

My mom worked as a receptionist, in department stores and Walmart. My dad was a truck driver and then had a towing business. He's a hustler; he started a bunch of "work for himself" projects. His follow-through wasn't always the best. He didn't always finish things, but he had an edge that said, "I'm not gonna have a boss" that pushed him to be self-employed. I'm not sure my dad even graduated from high school.

Was your family supportive of your efforts to do meaningful work or did they think traditional work was better for you?

My parents told me I had to learn a trade to earn a living. As a kid, I was always into art. I remember at four drawing dinosaurs and loving it. My mom encouraged me early on, but they said you can't make a living as an artist.

Tell us about your educational experience.

My early school years were good. Then we moved to Pennsylvania, and things got tough. I missed six months of school in the move. When I finally got back into school, I was nervous that I was gonna get left back. I soon realized that I was a year ahead of them. The kids and some of the teachers were bullies. I was the outsider and an easy target. I'd just wear my headphones and try to stay out of their way. I liked math, but it was hard to learn from a jerk.

I was able to get out of that school and into a vocational tech school where I studied printing. I wasn't that interested in printing, but it made my parents happy and made my school days tolerable. I did well in that program and graduated.

When I told my parents that I wanted to go to college, they said, "You're an idiot; you're gonna have loans to pay back." I felt discouraged but somehow ended up getting grants, scholarships, and work study. The local community college was a quality, well-funded school. I decided to try the video, audio, radio, and television program. It was cool, and I liked everything.

J's journey to finding meaningful work:

One thing I always loved was drawing. I won a competition in second grade and thought if I sold a picture to everybody in the world for a dollar, I'd be a millionaire. When I drew, I was "in the zone." I just kept drawing and drawing. I turned out weird stuff on the back of my math test: dinosaurs with math symbols for eyes. And then, in seventh/eighth grades, the message I heard was "you better get serious about your life, young man. You can't be an artist; that's just what flaky, wacko people do."

At fourteen I got my first job stocking shelves. My mom told me that work was like this. Doing the same thing over and over. I thought, there's no way I can do this every day for twenty years. I just can't. I tried a lot of part-time jobs like dishwashing in high school. I always had a job, and each one proved to be a good incentive for finding a way to go to college. Around this time, I started playing guitar, something I continued throughout my life. I was in a band in high school and continued while I was in college. Music was and still is important to me.

My work=study job was in the mailroom, and the guy I worked for changed my life. He was nicest dude I'd ever met. He was supportive of me and told me I wasn't stupid. I get chills thinking about how it felt to have someone believe in me. He told me, "Just be nice to people when you deliver the mail. That's part of your job—be nice to people." It's a lesson I carry with me today.

By the time I finished my first year of college, I was doing freelance jobs on top of school and the post office. I was definitely the go-getter kid along with the five other go-getter kids in class. We would team up and and shoot videos for weddings. I learned sound technology and enjoyed the work. I was learning in school, but when we did the gigs, I learned on the job. I would be nervous at first that I wouldn't figure it out, but I always did, so that helped build my confidence. I also worked in the print shop at the college, and the boss there was great too.

The band evolved in college. We wrote all our own music and were slowly getting better and finding gigs to play. We weren't earning much money, but we had fun. I could work a job where I felt valued and play music in my free time. I was pretty sure I could be a rock star because:

1. They existed; I could see people doing it for a living.
2. I loved it.
3. I couldn't imagine myself doing anything else.

After I graduated from community college, I kept working at the same job in the mailroom. Soon I was promoted to be the head of the audiovisual department. I had to choose, buy, install, and fix every piece of equipment at the college. In the mailroom, I worked with a bunch of people, and we had fun and worked hard. Now I was working alone; I was supposed to change the way I dressed; people expected me to be available all the time and then act like things were an emergency (when they weren't). It wasn't for me. Even though I was working in the job I was trained for, I went back to the mailroom full-time.

I was so happy to have money from working that I soon bought $2,000 worth of audio gear. It took all my savings, but I bought a real mixer and sampler. The band had been together for seven years, and everything was going great. We were actually playing shows pretty much every weekend around Pennsylvania. We even played CBGB's in New York. We decided we'd do a show on the campus and have an art show at the same time. We're playing this epic show, and all these young artists were showing their stuff, and this kid brings like the coolest sh*t I've ever seen. He painted on doors and then nailed stuff on right on it, whatever the hell he wanted. It was mad-crazy-person energy. I was blown away. That night my bandmate tells me he's leaving the next day to move to another state, and my girlfriend breaks up with me. What am I supposed to do now?

Within a few weeks, I run into crazy-person-energy artist guy. I ended up going to his house, and I was totally intimidated. I ended up painting with him, and he taught me so much, but three things in particular:

1. Paint with your hands; you'll expect nothing of yourself, and everything will be better than you think. It's like you're not even trying, but you're doing something. It's like playing

guitar with your feet.

2. Do what your brain tells you to do. If you argue with yourself, you'll go nuts.

3. Get rid of the crap, and all you will be left with is the good stuff. If you still don't like it, work over it.

My mission was to create one hundred paintings. Not, how am I going to sell these, or what should I paint that someone else would like? I wanted to free my brain up so I could learn to create. I painted every day. I finally showed my paintings to some friends just for the fun of it. I sold one. Then I figured out how to sell more. I would go around to various places and talk to shop owners. I went to a cool tattoo shop, and they said they would look at my paintings. I knew they might like my stuff, but I could see they'd probably also like drawings of skulls and dragons, so I made some. They loved the drawings and my art. They took the drawings and started to sell them for twenty-five dollars. I took the money from the tattoo shop and bought materials and started to create three-by-five-foot paintings. I got a book from the library on being an artist. I just kept going.

Today, I work full-time as a painter. I teach the lessons that I learned from crazy-person-energy guy. I'm amazed that I am where I am today, given where I came from.

Assess your strengths and weaknesses.

When you assess either your strengths or weaknesses, think about yourself the way you might a dear friend. We tend to be gentler, kinder, more thoughtful when we think about the positive and negative attributes of our friends. Take this approach to your own analysis.

Strengths

Pick three to five strengths that significantly differentiate you from your peers. When I would try to point out a strength to my kids, they would say, "You're my mom—you have to say that." They were probably right. But if some of the positive attributes your mom or dad has pointed out about you have also been stated by teachers or friends, there's a good chance they're right.

Here are some prompts to help get you started:

- What have others complimented you on?
- What do others come and ask you for help with?
- Which projects have you spent hours on without getting tired?
- What are some of your favorite activities and why?

Weaknesses

Pick three weaknesses that could be improved upon to help you be a better human. Don't be defensive. This is not an exercise in altering your personality. Note these traits in the way you might write your grocery list. As a reminder, the main reason you are doing this work is to improve your ability to find meaningful work. The assessment of both plusses and minuses is more useful when kept short and light; use a hairbrush, not a sledgehammer.

Here are some prompts to help get you started:

- What do you regularly need to ask someone else for help with?
- Which projects and tasks drain your energy?
- What are activities you avoid doing and why?

This is not an exercise in negative self-talk; the idea is to become more self-aware. Add a heaping helping of humility and self-compassion in your journey to understand yourself. Be honest with yourself but no beating yourself up—that would defeat everything we are trying to do here.

Seek Help

If you need help getting started, search online for a list of common strengths and weaknesses. If you need further help, ask a nonjudgmental friend, pastor, counselor, teacher, relative, etc., what they believe are your strengths and weaknesses and write down what they say. Act as if you are a journalist gathering information. Just because they are saying it doesn't make it true; each person you ask may be influenced by their own experiences and background. Do a gut check on what they are saying; maybe they said something that, in your heart, you know is valid.

Once you have outlined what you believe are your strengths and weaknesses, check them with someone you trust. I would suggest asking someone different from the person who helped you compile the list, if you used someone—probably not your mom or dad or any relative unless you are certain that they can be honest and will keep what you say confidential. A better choice might be a mentor. (See chapter 9.) This is a person you approach to help guide you through difficult decisions and act as a sounding board.

It may be hard to learn that someone perceives you as a know-it-all or angry or whatever. But it's far better to understand that this is how you are perceived so you can do something about it.

Current Skills and Skill Gaps Assessment

A skills assessment is equally important. Review your current skills and gaps and make a list of each. Pay particular attention to any gaps that you have identified. This list will evolve, but right now, there may be something you can work on. Even if right now isn't a good time to work on the gaps, keep the list where it is easy to refer to. The list might change, but your desire to improve your skill base is one thing that needs constant attention. These don't have to be "work" skills—they might be soft skills like communication or empathy or painting or singing. It doesn't matter what skill you want to improve, only that you are consciously working on what's important to you.

CHAPTER 5

KNOW YOUR PERSONAL VALUES

A few years ago, I was the speaker at a conference talking about the impact of millennials and Gen Z in the workplace. Before my talk, I was cornered by a CEO who relayed his experience interviewing and trying to hire someone from these age groups.

CEO: You need to hear my story; you're not going to believe it.
Me: OK.
CEO: So, I'm interviewing this kid, and they are nodding and listening. Their experience is a great fit for the job I have. I introduce them around. My colleagues are favorable. We go back to my office to discuss some final details. We sit down, and the kid turns to me and says, "Thank you very much for your time, but I'm going to end the interview at this point." I was completely shocked. No one has ever ended an interview with me before.
Me: Why did they end the interview?
CEO: I don't know. I was so angry I didn't really listen to what they said. You see how arbitrary they are, how self-centered?
Me: I can see why you were upset. I'm interested in learning more about why they ended the interview.
CEO: Well, they said something selfish about wanting, air quotes, balance in their life. That I had made it clear that everyone here works long hours and is expected to be here well into the evening. They said they weren't interested in that. See how lazy they are?
Me: With all due respect, I can see their point. Many millennials value their personal time above many other things. What they were telling you was that their values are not the same as us baby boomers'. Working sixty-plus hours a week with little time for family and fun is not what they want.
CEO: Well, that's just stupid. Don't they have any ambition? Don't they want to get ahead? How are they going to do that if they don't work hard?

At this point, I thanked the CEO for the story and said that I hoped he might gain something from my upcoming talk.

While I could understand the CEO's frustration, I equally understood the interviewee's perspective. This baby boomer boss assumed that their values were more important than the interviewee's. Rather than trying to understand what the interviewee valued and listening to their point of view, this hiring manager neglected to secure the services of a potentially valuable employee, all because they were unwilling to grasp what someone else valued.

I admired the interviewee for having the awareness to end the interview and not waste any more of their or the CEO's time. The interviewee actually did the CEO a favor by being honest. The CEO could have learned from them. Instead, the CEO was angry because they were unwilling to acknowledge the world through the perspective of a potentially great employee.

Maybe you can relate to this story; maybe it's your parents, your friends, or your coworkers who have used their values as a yardstick for your progress. I heard it over and over in my research for this book: "My parents just don't understand why I don't want to...

- ☙ work twelve-hour days;
- ☙ get ahead the way they did;
- ☙ give up so much of personal time in order to 'work.'"

They may never understand, but at least you have the satisfaction of knowing the basis for your path forward.

In this chapter, I hope you'll learn to identify the personal values that most significantly affect your work life. In part 2, you'll learn how to translate those values into finding meaningful work. The more you understand your values, the better you will be able to discern whether a job is a good fit for you.

Organizations Are Slow to Acknowledge Millennial and Gen Z Strengths

As acknowledged in the example at the beginning of this chapter, I have listened to baby boomer bosses complain about how millennials and Gen Zers *don't want to work hard,* how they *are entitled and always on their phones.* They mention how they *have to keep an eye on these younger employees because they are not as productive as older workers.* I was so distressed by this attitude that I developed the talk mentioned before to help leaders understand how the values of boomers and millennials and Gen Z diverge and how an organization can adapt to their attitudes and strengths at work.

Organizational digital transformation has been slow, and this has affected how well companies have adapted to changing employee requirements. While some companies have effectively changed—particularly those that have digital roots, such as Amazon and Google—others have paid the price of holding on to old ways of perceiving and motivating employees.

In the early 1990s, telecommuting allowed flexible work hours and places. Employees at more advanced companies could work remotely. These companies figured out that allowing employees to work from home would be beneficial not just to employees but also to their bottom line by lowering costs for office space. Other companies were afraid that employees would take advantage of being at home and that they would not be able to control what their employees did. Organizations that didn't transform failed to thrive. Failure of leadership is often not recognized until long after the changes should have taken place. Today, flexible work hours are common.

> "Being unclear about your values is a threat to your livelihood and well-being."

Maintaining Authenticity at Work

In addition to career aspirations, there is another compelling reason to be clear about your values. As you progress in your careers, people will want you to conform. When you don't, they may react aggressively. It's not easy to stand your ground in the face of an antagonistic authority figure. Particularly when it involves your paycheck.

Being unclear about you values is a threat to your livelihood and well-being. Maybe you know this from your own experience. The stress of being in the wrong job with the wrong people can take a toll.

In the CEO-interviewee example, if the interviewee had not been clear about their values, they might have taken that job and worked for someone who doesn't appreciate their key values. Think of personal values as vitamins. They may not change our health dramatically, but we'll feel better if we incorporate them into our daily lives. If we live according to what's important to us, our immune system will be stronger.

As you turn away from people and experiences that diminish you, you embrace those that support you. Comparing your values to someone else's is a waste of time. No one else has your genes, your family, and experiences. Values are embedded in who we are. They are shaped by our parents, our environment, our education, and our experiences.

Understanding your values is part of the journey to meaningful work; without the light of self-awareness, you search in the dark.

What Are Personal Values?

Personal values are those characteristics and behaviors that guide our decisions. While skills and strengths can be improved, values tend

"Understanding your values is part of the journey to meaningful work; without the light of self-awareness, you search in the dark."

to be a consistent and important part of us. Some people value competitiveness. For others, it's cooperation. Maybe you value adventure or status or money or helping others. Can you recognize how each of these shapes the kind of work you might do? One value leads to a dramatically different kind of work than another.

Sometimes the best way for us to know what our values are is to consider what other people value and test if their values fit us. This isn't comparing—my values are better than yours—it's using the power of relativity to learn abstract things about ourselves. If there were a computer we could plug in to, like a car-repair diagnosis computer, that might be useful. But no such thing exists. We're left with doing it step by step, one relationship, one job, one hobby at a time. The best way to evaluate the validity of our values list is to test them out in real life. These values are part of the equation that makes us who we are, and who we are is amazing.

MEANINGFUL CASE WORK STUDY

Where did you grow up?

I grew up in California, Colorado, and Atlanta, Georgia. My parents got divorced when I was a baby, so I would travel back and forth between each house during the holidays. I would spend half the summer and every other holiday with my dad and stepmom in Atlanta. I spent the school year with my mom, so most of my growing up was in Southern California.

What did your parents do for a living?

My dad worked for the US Forest Service and retired in 2014. My stepmom is an art teacher; she just entered semiretirement. My mom has worked in several places within natural resources and currently works with the US Forest Service. My stepdad writes permits for water quality and construction projects for the State of California.

How do you define meaningful work for yourself?

I define meaningful work as something that makes me feel accomplished and that has a tangible, positive impact either on someone or the environment. For me, working in marine science and being a field technician is meaningful work, which meant following a "traditional path" of attending college.

Tell us about your educational experience.

I am currently in graduate school pursuing a certificate in wildlife management with plans to pursue either a Master of Science in Natural Resources or Wildlife Sciences. My coursework focuses on conservation, species recovery, and policy.

M's journey to finding meaningful work:

I first became aware of my personal values in Montessori school.

I stood up to bullies and pushed back against social norms on the playground. My values and convictions got stronger when I moved to California and entered a new school system. Becoming aware of my personal values has impacted my career journey by giving me a critical eye about who I apply to work with, where I would want to be stationed/live for work, and how my work impacts my larger goals.

A low point in my work journey was when I was working as a resident assistant at college. For almost two straight months, residents from my and other dorms opened up to me about being suicidal. This was taking a toll on me. I was burning the candle at both ends and felt incredibly stressed, doing my best to support my residents, take care of myself, and do well in my classes. I realized I couldn't do everything and couldn't maintain my own commitments, if I didn't say no and carve out specific time for myself.

I found a recent job through USAJOBS.gov. The work my crewmates and I did was critical to preserving habitat for fish and other wildlife. However, I wasn't happy while doing it because of the toxic work environment and suffering from chronic pain flare-ups with no proper treatment.

This was mostly composed of toxic masculinity (perpetuated by both men and women), fragile masculinity, misogyny, and disregard for other people's safety. Some examples were: people bragging about how broken and bruised their bodies were at the end of a field day/week, comparing each other's pain/looking down on you if you spend all day in the office versus field, using an *R* slur, and smoking marijuana in close quarters even after I mentioned being deathly allergic to it. I was around people who were bigoted and misgendering me throughout the season. I did not feel safe to be my authentic self. When not in work environments, I was isolated from some social events too.

A high point was the internship I did in the summer of 2017 with the Geospatial Ecology of Marine Megafauna Lab. I was a research intern on a gray-whale-foraging ecology project, and it was the first time I was doing what I dreamed of doing as a child: working on the ocean and watching for whales every day. It made my heart sing, even when conditions weren't the best, I still enjoyed every day. That experience taught me a lot about being open to different outcomes and what I want in a boss and in a team.

What do you envision for your future work?

My ideal coworkers are folks who know how to balance work,

social responsibilities, and relationships; who are open-minded, have integrity, and a good work ethic.

My dream job would be working as part of a research team doing a monitoring project with cetaceans (specifically, killer whales) and doing photo identification. In a broader view, I'd want to be a part of any interesting marine or wildlife research project.

I'd want to have a positive, respectful relationship with my boss. Someone who takes initiative and does their best to be approachable. I want a boss who praises employees both publicly and privately.

I want a positive and encouraging work culture where people don't feel pressured to compromise their health, mentally and physically. I want to work with folks who enjoy being there and doing their work.

I've learned that even if I am not satisfied with the overall job, I find joy in the small things. I enjoy "menial" office work because it allows me to be independent and assist the team in achieving the goal through less glamourous ways. I may not be trekking the farthest, but I am making some of the most detailed maps and reports a crew leader can ask for. I find joy in completing tasks that have been on the backburner because it means we can focus on the larger, more exciting tasks.

When employed with the US Forest Service, I took advantage of the weekly free training courses and gained a basic skill set in ArcGIS, which is a skill that employers often ask for in my field. For me, taking advantage of educational opportunities is key to succeeding. I also do my best to stay up-to-date on first aid/CPR and other free certifications like the boat handling license. Several of my potential jobs/career fields require a level of physical fitness, so I work out consistently to be as fit as I can for those jobs.

The two things that concern me the most are my developing limitations due to my chronic pain flare-ups and the potential of being passed over/fired for being a member of the LGBTQIA+ community. A salient phrase for me is "to be openly queer is to choose your happiness over your safety." I often "go back in the closet" so I can be hired and only come out and take my mask off when I've assessed that it's safe to do so.

Understand your values.

Think back on a major decision you made in the last six months. It doesn't have to be "life changing," just one that had some consequences that you realize in hindsight.

How much time did you devote to that decision? What values did you weigh in the pros and cons? Were the values related to your time? Your money? Your friends?

I recommend that you take a few minutes right now and jot down a few notes about how your values influence the choices you make—and if they don't, maybe you don't hold those factors as values, or maybe you need to reevaluate how you make decisions.

Here are a few situations to consider as you get ready to think about what you value:

- Why are you friends with your best friend?
- Why do you live where you live right now?
- Why do you work where you are employed right now?
- How do you determine how you spend your free time?

Now, read through the following table of values. Feel free to add values not on this list; it's just there to jump-start your thinking. Pick eight to twelve that reflect what seems important to you. It may not be easy to narrow the list, but it's important. Too many values will be hard to manage when you're making decisions about work. Ideally, you'll narrow again—choose five or six values that capture your core. Rely on your intuition to compare and rank the values on your list.

Don't stress over this. There are no right or wrong answers. Trust your gut and don't let your logical brain interfere too much. Do not judge your list. Values are unique and relative to each of us.

If you are struggling, find someone objective to talk with. Pick someone who won't try to influence you. The last thing we need when we are doing this work is someone else's judgment. Trust yourself.

A List of Core Values

There are a lot of value lists online. Here are some common values to get you started.

Abundance	Accountability	Achievement	Action
Adventure	Ambition	Awareness	Balance
Beauty	Being the Best	Calmness	Cheerfulness
Clarity	Comfort	Compassion	Competition
Connection	Contribution	Control	Courage
Creativity	Curiosity	Determination	Discipline
Effectiveness	Empathy	Energy	Enthusiasm
Excellence	Fairness	Faith	Fame
Family	Flexibility	Freedom	Friendship
Fulfillment	Fun	Harmony	Happiness
Health	Honesty	Honor	Humility
Independence	Integrity	Intelligence	Intimacy
Inspiration	Kindness	Knowledge	Liveliness
Love	Money	Nature	Passion
Peace	Perfection	Persistence	Philanthropy
Power	Respect	Security	Simplicity
Significance	Spirituality	Spontaneity	Strength
Stability	Success	Status	Teamwork
Tolerance	Tradition	Truth	Vitality
Wealth	Wisdom		

My Family Values

As you review your list, note whether your values apply equally to your personal life and professional life. My experience is that they tend to be similar. For instance, doing this exercise a long time ago helped me understand what values I wanted to instill in my children. As an example of the power this You Work It exercise can have, I'll now share how I talked to my kids about education and work—after I sorted out my own values.

Education

I have a master's degree and value education, and yet I understand that college isn't for everyone (see chapter 7 for tools to help you determine if further academic study is for you)—nor is a formal education necessary for every job. Think of a school bus driver. They have a very important job: transporting our children. It's important to me to appreciate every person's work journey, regardless of whether it includes a lot of education. Here are the messages I tried to relay about education to my children:

- Love to learn. One reason parents of young children are told to read to their kids is that the love of reading and learning is not innate in everyone. It needs to be taught and nurtured.
- Learn how to learn. School is good for exposing children to a wide variety of subjects. We get opportunities to be exposed to things that we might otherwise miss. It is important to know how to study, how to focus, how to get things done.
- College isn't for everyone. College can be useful for providing us with a transformational experience, if we put energy into the experience. It isn't right for everyone. A college degree used to be considered a career necessity. For the past seventy-five years, a degree was a way for corporations to have good soldiers for the corporate army. It would weed out anyone who didn't fit the mold. I followed this path and don't regret it. But to tell young people that college is the best or only way to succeed is ludicrous. There are many ways to contribute to society and earn a good living that have nothing to do with college.

Now, college isn't just about the book learning or mastering a major; it's also about meeting people who are different from us. It's learning from teachers who have had broad experiences and bring perspectives that enrich us. For example, at community college, I had a German teacher who had left Germany in the 1930s when Hitler was rising to power. He later joined the US Army and marched into his German hometown as part of the liberation forces. Imagine the power of that experience as it translates into how this man taught me German—and how I received the language lessons.

Work

Work is necessary to live, and it was important to me that my family learn to be independent. The freedom to choose how and where one lives is dependent on being able to support oneself. Financial independence is a key to having choices that can lead to happiness. For example, I didn't allow myself to get stuck doing things I didn't want to do; I made sure I had the means to change jobs by earning enough money to take care of myself. I don't mean you should never ask for or get help, but I do mean that you are responsible for your own way in the world.

- **Find a way to do something you enjoy in order to support yourself.** We spend not just our limited time working but our creativity, our humanity, and our spirit. If we spend our days doing draining work, we rob ourselves of the chance to contribute and thrive.
- **Build work that serves your needs.** I imagine each of you has something that you love to do that isn't work. Maybe you have children or play soccer. Work is a part of your life; it is not your life. This may be easy for you to understand, but what's tricky is earning a good living while keeping these interests in mind. My challenge was to build flexibility into my schedule in a corporate environment that didn't offer it. The balance of money and time is tricky. I wanted my children to understand that it's up to them to decide for whom they work, how they work, and what they do for work.
- **Build a big bag of skills and interests.** Get exposed to lots of skills and activities so you know what you like and don't like. Know what energizes you. A limited background may serve some, but as a rule, having a broader set of skills and experiences increases choices. With more alternatives, it's easier to manage your energy (physical activity), your psyche (emotional and psychological needs), and your soul

(spiritually, what keeps you balanced).

- ◈ **Be coachable.** It's important to be able to learn how to be coached. Playing sports is just one way to learn this. I didn't have the opportunity growing up, and I think I missed out on learning important skills early. Team-related activities teach important skills like listening to a coach or teacher in order to improve. We may think of coaching as something that comes with athletics, but coaching can come in many forms. The chess club or yearbook committee can be great practice for being directed. You may find a coach at a volunteer job. The idea is not to be cocky or too sure of yourself. Meaningful work will require an open mind and heart. The best way to stay humble is to know that you will be able to learn something from everyone. Think about times when you were a good student (not in the classroom sense but in the life sense). Pay attention to the circumstances, your state of mind, and the person you learned from. What did you bring to the relationship? What were your interactions with your "coach" like? Hopefully, this practice helps you think about other ways you can improve your coachability.

CHAPTER 6

ASSESS YOUR CURRENT "WORK"

I f you haven't already discovered through reading an earlier chapter in this book, it's easier to figure out where you want to go if you have a clear picture of where you are now. The hard part about seeing your current situation clearly is that...you're in the middle of it! You have limited perspective. Understanding both how you feel and what you think about your current work situation takes fresh eyes.

One place to start is by noting what you've learned about yourself in earlier chapters—your skills, the gaps you want to fill, and your key values. If it's been a while since you've reviewed your notes on those topics, take time to do that now. If you didn't do that work yet (see chapters 4 and 5 for some guidance), I hope you will take time now to jot some things down.

Without doing this work, trying to assess your current situation is like driving from New York to Philadelphia without your GPS. You will get there, but it will be frustrating and take longer. Of course, you might get lucky, but it would be just that—luck. It's unlikely that you'd be able to learn anything useful for future trips.

And that's what we're about to do now—take a new trip. One that explores your current job.

PART 1

Rate your current job.

Rate your current job on a scale of 1 to 10:

1 = I should have left here a long time ago.

10 = This job is a perfect fit for me right now.

Don't linger over an answer; go with your gut and respond quickly. You can examine your thoughts and feelings later. Right now, we want to get a picture of your satisfaction and fit with this current opportunity.

What about the job makes you rate it this way? Consider:

- How you got this job (personal connection, online, etc.)
- How long you've been at the job
- What you like the most
- What you like the least
- The work environment
- How empowered you feel to do your work in a way that is meaningful to you

I hope these considerations nudge you to write down other things that are positive and negative about your current situation. You don't need pages and pages, but writing things down is helpful to dig out hidden feelings and thoughts.

You can start using this information right away, or you can put this personal assessment away for a few days. When you take it back out and review it, some things may pleasantly surprise you. Some things might bother you more than you expected. The goal is that you begin to form a picture of how you are, at this job, in this organization, right now.

What Is Your Pattern?

If you've had more than three jobs in the past one to two years, think about what criteria you used for leaving each gig. If you've been in a job for more than a year and hate it, review your criteria for staying. There is nothing wrong with staying or changing. What matters is why.

If you are staying in a job because you can't think of what else to do or if you continue to leave jobs after a few months, assess yourself in your current job in these categories:

- **Attitude**—Do you have a "good" or "bad" attitude? You know the truth. If it's good, then you probably like your job. If your attitude is negative, there may be lots of reasons why. Identify the difference between what belongs to other people and what belongs to you. Write down the three to five sticking points of the job. Then assess whether you are contributing to the problem. Are you reacting from an emotional place? Emotions are important to understand. Remember: It's not personal; it's business. This saying might irk you, but it's true. A lot of the time, decisions "against" us aren't personal. Often, they have nothing to do with us. We may have to live with the consequences, but it's not about us. Be prepared to let go of comments that may seem like personal attacks. Many times, the other person lashing out is working something out internally; it's not about us. I suggest you don't own all the comments, good and bad, that are tossed your way. Even when it is personal, we do not have to accept unacceptable behavior. Navigating those waters is tricky; get help if you find yourself in one of those situations.
- **Contribution**—How do you feel about the work you do? Do you feel like your contribution makes any difference? Does it matter to you if your contribution is valued? If not, skip to another criterion.
- **Boss**—Are you learning from this person? If yes, what are you learning? Is this the kind of learning that is important to you? Do you check in regularly on how you're doing? You may be learning how not to be a boss. That's valuable too.
- **Colleagues**—Do you feel that you are valued by your colleagues? Do you feel part of a team? Is a team environment important to you? Do you value your interaction with them? Do you want a more social group? Write down what you like and dislike about working with these people.
- **Work environment**—Related to colleagues, what kind of environment do you work in? Is it casual? Rigid? Are the benefits good for you? Or does the organization offer lots of things that you don't care about? How about flexibility,

assignments, hierarchy?

- **Chances to learn**—Is this important to you? Do you know what you want to learn? Have you discussed this topic with your boss? Is it clear that the organization is committed to continuous learning? If not, how does the organization treat those who learn and take risks?

- **Opportunities to advance**—Did you ask questions about advancement in the hiring process? If yes, what have you learned about advancement at this company? Have you identified internal jobs that you might like, and have you identified someone to take over your work if you get an opportunity to move up? This is important because having an idea of who can do your work will help you move seamlessly to your new gig.

- **Compensation**—Is the company financially stable? Is your pay in line with your skills and contribution? We can all use more money. But more money won't necessarily make us happy. There's a threshold, however, of money that we are comfortable with; if your pay is too far below that threshold, you are likely to be unhappy.

What did you learn from this assessment of your current gig? This is a good time for an intuitive gut check.

Should You Stay, or Should You Go Now?

For most of us, the decision to stay or go is complicated. These are just a few of the influences:

- Money—Can I afford to change?
- Time—If I stay (my job isn't that bad), will I get behind where I want to be in my career and/or personal life? Time is ticking...
- Outside opinions—What will others (family/friends) think if I change jobs (again)?

You have your own reasons and ideas about staying or switching. It is important to be clear about your reasons. I use the following three criteria (in addition to financial compensation) for judging whether I should take on any work (paid or volunteer).

- **Am I learning?** The more clearly you understand what

you want to learn (I recommend writing down the kind of experiences you want to have), the more likely it is that you will be able to find a way to ask if that experience is open to you. If you want to learn more about supervising people or financials or project management, you can learn about that topic on your own and/or ask your supervisors if and how you can learn these skills at your job.

- **Am I appreciated?** This doesn't equate to just pay and benefits. Think about all the ways that an employer shows appreciation. Did you get the flexible schedule that you asked for? Do you get recognized in front of your peers? Do others get recognized? There are hundreds of ways for an organization to show appreciation.
- **Am I having fun?** You know when an activity is fun. I don't mean laughing out loud every minute; I mean, time flies when you're there. You feel good about your contribution and the people you work with.

You don't need to have positive responses to all three of these, but I do recommend you have two of the three.

I've found this to be an easy way to objectively assess the fitness of a given situation to gauge if it serves me or not. These may not be the important criteria for you. If not, develop your own list. It can change over time. If you are struggling to select criteria, try using mine or go back to the list of questions that you answered in the self-assessment. Hopefully, some things will jump out at you there. No specific criteria are good or bad. It only matters that you understand what is important to you.

PART 2

Pretend to quit your job.

Here's another fun exercise to try: pretend you just gave notice at your current gig.

I'm not suggesting you really quit your job; this is just to check what comes up for you. You could even write a sample resignation letter.

How do you feel? Are you freaking out? Are you relieved? Do another gut check. What is it telling you?

Always Be Looking

One last tip: always be looking for new jobs, no matter how much you enjoy the job you're in. There are a few reasons to do this:

- ❦ It helps build connections.
- ❦ It aids in keeping your eyes open for opportunities for you and your connections.
- ❦ No matter how stable your current gig seems, you never know what changes lie ahead. The more prepared you are for changes, the less you will be victimized by the whims of business (and life).

I am not saying always be changing jobs. I'm saying always be looking. You deserve work that feeds you. But as we all know from our own experiences, finding work that serves us and a life that supports us as we are is hard work.

CHAPTER 7

SHOULD YOU GO BACK TO SCHOOL?

You may be asking yourself this complicated question. School always seems like a safe choice. Parents may say that more schooling is always worth it. I understand their perspective. Many of them came of age in a time when middle-class families had limited access to higher education (and it was not accessible for most lower-class families). The boomer experience is that college is the key to success. Studies show that college does increase earnings over a person's career.[14] My sympathy, however, lies with the person who isn't sure what to study or that spending four years of their life and $100,000+ will get them work that is meaningful to them.

To begin, this chapter discusses traditional college environments, but later in the chapter, we add the spectrum of opportunities beyond "higher education," including:

- Career schools, for example, schools in culinary arts, the trades, aeronautics, and health sciences—these include certificate programs and technical licenses.
- Apprenticeships that pay you while you learn a trade, such as carpenter, electrician, or plumber.

You might be thinking, *I'm not interested in those.* That's OK, but maybe you know someone who is. Or maybe when you look back at what you loved as a kid; you'll remember you loved, for instance, to take things apart. Maybe being an engineer isn't for you but being an electrician would be. If you consider your values and skills, including what you might want to learn, you might make unexpected discoveries.

The Risks of College

College...
- is expensive and has helped create a student-debt burden of over a trillion dollars;[15]

* no longer guarantees a job, with the exception of a few fields; and
* may not offer you the kind of college "experience" that is worth the cost. Many academic environments still have students spending most of their time sitting in classrooms being lectured to by faculty who may or may not have worked recently outside of academia. Alternatively, while I support remote learning, sitting in front of a computer for several hours a day is not the same as being on campus, meeting people from different backgrounds.

The Benefits of College

Despite the negatives, positive reasons to return to school exist. Here are some arguable ideas:

* Education is never wasted. Being exposed to a broad swath of people and educational experiences has lifelong value. The connections you make in college may lead to friendships and opportunities down the road.
* Education can be transformational. Hopefully for most people, studying and learning a subject in-depth is a powerful experience. We enter school one kind of person and leave, some years later, changed. The world becomes alternatively smaller and larger. We gain respect for doers and thinkers alike.
* Whether your degree ever gets you a job or not, you will have the personal satisfaction of completing this journey. In addition, long into the future, there will be people for whom the extended educational credential is meaningful, and this will separate you from others applying for an opportunity.

My Personal Feeling about Grad School

I have a master's degree. It's been many years since that degree has influenced my job selection or which job selected me. My advanced degree didn't matter to many employers. All they wanted to know was that I had a degree. Frankly, my degree barely supplied me with any of the tools I needed to do the job I was hired for directly out of school. But the fact that I had a degree showed my employer that I had checked a box. One of their highly rated boxes. The need or desire for this type credential may diminish in the coming years, but in the past, having that degree opened certain doors.

If you choose to go to graduate school, I hope you will study something you love. You have to spend a lot of time thinking about, being absorbed in, and regurgitating whatever you study. You'll get a job somehow; you'll figure that out. But spending precious time and money doing something because you should or because someone else wants you to will be problematic.

And Now...a Story

CHRIS EVALUATES THEIR GIG

Chris tried college. They studied history, the only subject that interested them. After struggling for two years, Chris dropped out and got a job as a server in a high-end restaurant. Chris liked the restaurant business and had a knack for pleasing customers. Also, knowing that they weren't a "sit in an office all day" person, Chris was pleased to find that the money was much better than other early-career jobs. Chris learned quickly from more experienced servers that showing up on time and taking other people's shifts when needed was a way to impress the boss. But Chris was looking for ways to learn and move up, and while the restaurant group had twelve locations, Chris discovered that there wasn't an easy path to more responsibility.

Chris got used to the money, so finding a different kind of job with the same hours, income, and career preparation wasn't easy. They felt stuck. Chris weighed their options:

★ Stay at the restaurant and keep pushing for advancement.
★ Leave the restaurant and find a "regular" 9-to-5 job.
★ Work at the restaurant part-time and go back to school.

None of these options appealed to Chris, so they took a step back and thought. From their skills assessment, Chris knew that they wanted or needed to:

★ learn about running a business, specifically, financials, how to keep track of expenses, what to spend on marketing, etc.,
★ find a workplace where they could continuously learn, and
★ have a flexible schedule.

In comparing this list to their current job, Chris could tell that the scheduling need was being met, but beyond that, the job was missing some important criteria. Another factor that Chris weighed was to pay off the debt they had incurred in just two years of college. Taking on work with limited income wasn't an option. Getting out of debt was a priority. Here is the process that Chris then followed:

1. Chris considered going back to school but was unclear about what to study and was reluctant to incur further debt. One thing Chris hadn't done was investigate online classes. Unclear about what was being offered and costs, they decided to take the time to investigate options.
2. They had never considered working at a start-up. Chris's assumption was that the pay was terrible, and while they might be able to learn, the "cost" of losing income seemed to outweigh the benefits.
3. Chris decided to ask to their friends and acquaintances what steps they were taking to find opportunities. They decided to do this in a systematic way by building a spreadsheet of their connections and their ideas and approaches. With an open mind, Chris built an interesting list of alternative future paths. This list would serve not just the upcoming transition but those in the future. Chris made no judgments about what people told them; they just documented all the ideas.

WHAT CHRIS LEARNED

The most important thing they learned was that they had a lot of preconceived ideas about school, work, volunteering, start-ups, freelancing, etc. Before they started this assessment, they were automatically dismissing interesting alternatives. They learned that connecting and listening to other people's approaches was valuable.

Chris also found out that opportunities were all around. They narrowed their choices to the following:

★ Working for a small food-waste recycling company that needed help getting new customers. They wouldn't be able to pay much, but they needed some part-time sales help.
★ Earning a certificate by taking online courses in restaurant financial management. The certificate program was significantly less expensive and more practical than typical

college courses; it was a three-month program that would take about ten hours a week.
★ The local community college had a food service program. Most of the students were high school dropouts who had an aptitude in the culinary arts. The program was seeking mentors to work a few hours a month.

Similar ideas outside of food service were also abundant. Without clarity of what they wanted to learn; Chris would have been overwhelmed. Chris learned that it was equally important to know themselves and to be open to opportunities.

Alternatives to Going to College or Grad School

The world of education has shifted over the past ten to fifteen years. The opportunity to learn almost anything is now available online. Here are three trends in education that can influence how we fill skill gaps.

1. **MOOCs**, or Massive Open Online Courses (mooc.org), are free online courses from academic and other sources. Offerings such as MicroMasters® and professional certificates can help upgrade skills without the cost and time of traditional programs.

2. **Micro-credentialing**[16] addresses the issue of accreditation. One of the dilemmas of an online education is accreditation. Without the "blessing" of an acknowledged expert organization, students and employers have no way of judging the quality of the coursework and method of learning and assessment. Micro-credentials are scaled-down blocks of education that fill a skill gap. These include:

   ❦ Online courses from specific institutions
   ❦ Bootcamp certificates
   ❦ Apprenticeships from traditional universities or other resource
   ❦ Online learning platforms like Coursera (coursera.org), EdX (edx.org), and Udacity (udacity.com)

3. **Upskilling**[17] covers a wider variety of workers and skills than reskilling (training employees whose jobs have become obsolete to use their existing skills for a specific new job). Upskilling also helps workers build on their current skills to create work that meets future job requirements. While reskilling has largely been

done by a company or industry, upskilling is gaining attention from a broader coalition of partners.

4. **Makerspaces/Hackerspaces** (makerspaces.com) are creative, collaborative workspaces located in schools, public libraries, or other community facilities. They are dedicated to learning, exploring, and teaching a wide variety of skills, from crafting to programming to robotics. There are as many skills being taught as there are makerspaces. Schools from K–12 to universities are integrating makerspaces into their curriculum. In 2017, most libraries offered some level of Maker program.[18] Degrees, certificates, and transfer programs are available.

5. **Bluprint** (myblueprint.com) is a subscription-based on-demand video service for learning crafts such as quilting and jewelry-making. While these programs may not offer a "license," they can be a useful way to learn new or to update skills. You never know when these skills might come in handy.

6. **Trade schools** can help fill a skills gap.[19] They include an incredibly wide variety of programs, from traditional trades like auto repair and carpentry to fire safety and culinary arts. Health care jobs will continue to be in demand—think about dental hygienists, medical transcriptionists, as well as elderly caregivers. While many of these professions have lost "stature" to "academic" programs, work in the trades can be highly rewarding and creative work for many of us.

It can be challenging to decide which skill to upgrade or learn. Once you have an idea about which skill you want, search broadly for ways to fill the gap. It's important to seek out alternatives when thinking about knowledge or skill gaps.

MEANINGFUL CASE
WORK STUDY

 O

Where did you grow up?

New York City area. My parents immigrated to the US from Central America before I was born.

What did your parents do for a living?

My dad was a superintendent of a senior citizen building. My mom bounced back and forth between nannying and working in health care as a customer care coordinator. Since neither of them had the chance to study for a college degree, education was very important to them. They really wanted me to become a doctor.

Tell us about your educational experience.

I struggled in middle school, but then in high school, I started hanging out with the "smart" kids and became motivated to do well. That was a big change for me. I got scholarships and ended up going to a private university in upstate New York. I enrolled in premed and got Cs in my chemistry and biology classes. I changed majors to math and did much better. I finished college with a degree in math.

As a result of the recession of 2008, I decided I should try getting an MBA. I spent six months studying for the GMAT exam [a standardized test often required for admission by many business schools]. I applied and wasn't accepted, but I decided to try again. I received an email from MIT that they wanted me to retake a few undergrad courses. I did that, reapplied, got an interview, and ended up getting wait-listed because everyone who was laid off was now going back to school. I did get accepted into another good business school. I decided that instead of spending all this money on business school, I would strike out on my own and start a business.

O's journey to finding meaningful work:

My main job in college was working in the university's admissions office, which led to my first position out of college, working as a college engineering school admissions officer, recruiting students who were underperforming in high school. The school wanted to give students who might not seem like good candidates due to low SAT scores or grades a chance in college. Over 90 percent of the students ended up graduating from the program within four to five years with over 3.0 GPAs. It is interesting to look back and see that my work in education would provide a foundation for the work I do today.

I tested a few other ideas with limited success. I learned that I didn't like working by myself. I felt most comfortable when I worked with a team. This was an important lesson for me. I decided to take a course in entrepreneurship at the local community college, since I knew I wanted my own business. This led me to write my first business plan. That start-up provided a platform for high school or early-undergraduate engineering students to document their projects. There was nothing else like it available at the time. We failed because it took a long time to get people to pay for the service.

That failure led me to the next company I built, which is the one I have now. My business partner and I interviewed over one hundred people before deciding on our next venture. Our idea was to teach hobbyists and kids how to build different types of devices, whether it be a robot or a drone. We would then ship customers a different project in the mail, and then they could watch our prerecorded videos on our website teaching them how to build everything from start to finish. We launched it as part of a Kickstarter campaign, thinking that if we could make the crowdfunding campaign successful, it would help us validate the market and potentially give us a starting customer base. Our original goal was $25,000. We were shocked that by the end of the campaign we had raised $295,760!

The company is now four years old. We have pivoted three times, most recently as a result of the coronavirus pandemic. We originally sold our kits to parents who wanted fun, educational projects for their kids. That was tough, so we started selling to schools. When all the schools closed, we went back to selling to parents with live-streamed lessons.

How do you define meaningful work for yourself?

Meaningful work to me is having a purpose; the work I put out there has to help other people. I have to be having some kind of impact on the world. I also need to be making money to support myself, and it has to be something that I know I'm really good at.

I find that when those three things are aligned, I could be in the darkest moments of the business but still feel really good about where I am because all those things are in place.

Is there anything else you would like to tell us regarding your thoughts and feelings about finding and enjoying meaningful work?

It's interesting how I learned so much from my failures. I don't mind calling them failures—I've always been comfortable with that word. Almost studying to become a doctor, failing in my first few businesses, almost going to MIT, barely missing a chance to be part of a prestigious accelerator all felt like failure at the time. But then the Kickstarter thing happened, and it was finally like, wow, all the effort actually does pay off in the end. That's when I thought, OK, I can do this; I'm just going to keep going.

I would encourage people to find something that puts pep in their step. Always be learning. Plunge right in, even if you don't think you can swim; just give yourself the shot. If you sink, you'll eventually learn to swim.

Get honest about your education.

If you are identifying with this chapter and feel the need to explore, I hope you'll open your heart and mind to the world of available choices. Here's one way to start:

- Make a list of the three classes in school you loved and at least one or two you hated. The ones you love will help reveal who you are. The ones you hated will help you understand what you dislike and can point you to weaknesses or skill gaps.
- Review your work throughout this part of the book, paying attention to your skill gaps or jobs you might want to pursue. The goal is not to match a specific skill to a specific educational program but rather to document some general ideas you might return to as you consider your choices.
- Consider why you want to go back to school. Be honest with yourself. Are you considering it because you don't know what else to do or because your family expects you to? Use the information from the work you've done previously in this book to identify something that revs you up. If nothing jumps out from this exercise, talk it over with someone. Be sure to write things down in your notebook, if you're keeping one. Writing down ideas, thoughts, questions, and affirmations gives your subconscious a chance to guide you. Do you really need that degree, or do you feel compelled because it's what others have done or expect you to do?

As you think about what you might try, be sure to search online for alternative ideas, programs, and classes to build skills. Since the COVID-19 pandemic has moved a lot of in-person activities online, I expect the availability of online alternatives to blossom.

When important people in your life ask you why you are or are not going back to school, you might say something like "I understand you are concerned for my future, and I appreciate that. I'm weighing my options and will let you know when I'm closer to understanding what choices are right for me."

Own your unique, authentic self.

I consider this one of the most important self-assessments in the book. I've left it until the end of part 1 because I hope by now you understand the values and other factors that make you who you are. If you skipped chapter 1, I've included that core message here too.

Start listing ways you feel you naturally shine—not necessarily skills or strengths or values, just what makes you purely you.

For example, making order out of chaos is one of my most important self-definers. It's part value and part skill, and it encompasses who I am—I like a good challenge and to solve complex problems.

Here are some other examples:

- ❦ I make a great omelet.
- ❦ I love to make people feel safe and heard.
- ❦ I love to take things apart and put them back together.
- ❦ I'm funny.

The goal is to identify your specialness. Authenticity at work comes from self-awareness plus courage to act on that knowledge. Your list may include one or twenty ideas. If you need a boost, ask your friends, coworkers, family...anyone who knows you (and whom you trust).

This is meant to inspire you. If you find yourself struggling or feeling judgy of yourself, stop. Leave all this here. Go dance or sing or run outside. When you're ready, come back with an attitude of self-appreciation and get to work.

PART 2: OUTER WORK

I n part 1, you closely examined who you are—where you've been from a work perspective and where you are today. I hope you'll take some time to reflect on your journey by going through some of the You Work It exercises in that section of the book. Knowing yourself is vital to finding meaningful work.

Now, in part 2, we are going to consider your connection to the world outside of yourself—the ever-important connections you have with others. We'll also explore job alternatives like freelancing and entrepreneurship. Don't forget to explore the You Work It exercises and take inspiration from the case studies in this part too.

CHAPTER 8

THE POWER OF COMMUNITY

B eyond our common need for relationships, connections help us identify opportunities for growth and meaning. The process of making and keeping connections is a lifelong journey, sometimes made more difficult by modern living. Thanks to our digital and virtual connections, we are more aware of what is happening in the world than ever before. However, overwhelming amounts of information can strain our ability to feel like we belong.

Here are a few examples of how virtual connection can make us feel disconnected:

- Social media—The very tool that makes us think that we are connected to a large community can hinder our ability to have real connection.
- FOMO—The fear of missing out is common these days. Since we are exposed to so many ideas and people, we feel we should have a "better" life, car, relationship, etc. Social media leads to comparison. As we compare our insides (how we feel) to other people's outsides (how they look on, for example, Instagram), we feel "less than."
- Devices over living—Constantly checking our devices removes us from the moment. We can get the "feeling" of belonging from devices but without real-life reinforcement.
- Enforcing a bubble—We are born into an ecosystem. While digital connections can help us expand, they can also limit us if we generally include people who come from our same religion, race, or gender orientation; socioeconomic class or profession; and political orientation or geographic identification.

When we notice the diversity of our collective connections, we may find an opportunity to expand beyond our current comfort level. Look at your digital connections with an eye for diversity. Make a conscious effort to expand.

It Is Better to Give than to Get

Consistently connecting is also known as "activating" your network. A network is an active group focused on growing professionally. Many of us have hundreds of connections. We may feel comfortable reaching out to that group for help, but how much do we know about how we can help them? Keeping in contact with the purpose of knowing that person's professional goals differentiates a network connection from a personal one. (Of course, our personal connections can also be professional.)

If on Facebook all we do is see who is having a baby or who is vacationing, that isn't the kind of information that is likely to serve us for the purpose of finding meaningful work. Let me reiterate: having a social network on Facebook or Instagram can be good, but do not fool yourself into thinking that because you have two hundred, five hundred, or seven hundred connections, you have a network who will help you in your search for work. Likely several people there could serve this purpose, but unless you actively work your connections for ways you can help them, you don't have a network. It takes intention to activate these individuals beyond the personal.

I am disappointed when I receive an email from someone I barely know asking me for a favor. Typically, the person writes, "I know it's unlikely that you will help me, but I thought I would ask," implying there's no harm in asking. For me, there is harm in asking. It demonstrates a lack of awareness and caring on their part. It makes me wonder if all they do is use people. As a rule, I don't help someone who approaches me this way. I realize the individual is just "taking a chance" by asking, but to me, it's selfish.

A community is built through mutual respect. Be sure that if you ask someone for help, you are aware of the gift you are being given. Taking people for granted is not the way to build a useful network. Know the person you are asking for help. If you don't know them, offer them something that you think might be of value to them. At the very least, be aware—it is better to give than to get.

The Smartphone Dilemma

Recently, I was watching a special on Morocco in northern Africa. It featured a huge market square where hundreds of people were gathered (pre-COVID-19) to socialize, shop, have a beverage, etc. As the camera panned, no one was on their phone. They were laughing and chatting. The people in the marketplace were there to connect to people, in person. On purpose!

The more time we spend on our phones, the more we may ignore human beings and the more likely we are to miss important connections. In your search for meaningful work, I hope you will commit to spending time and energy consciously creating your network and community.

In this chapter, we explore the why we need each, how to give to get, and how to get over the distaste for networking (unless you're one of the rare people who love it!).

The Difference Between a Network and a Community

A **network** is a group of individuals who help us find our way through the world of work. Each of us needs a lot of support to travel this road. We travel this route from thirty to more than fifty years. In that time, we meet a lot of people. How many of those people can be plugged in to our network of colleagues, where the goal is to help each other succeed, however each of us defines success?

"In your search for meaningful work, I hope you will commit to spending time and energy consciously creating your network and community."

A **community** includes all the people in our life who contribute to our journey, whether that has to do with work or not. The challenge today is to create a large enough community so that we have support for our different needs—physical, emotional, spiritual, and psychological. The more fully we live our lives, the more we broaden our personal community.

Here is an illustration of the relationship between our community and our network. The most important part of this concept is to understand that there is a difference between our community and network. One is relatively passive (our community), and one is active when it comes to helping us find meaningful work. Being aware of the difference is useful.

Relationship Between Network and Community

ANYONE

People can flow back and forth.

NETWORK
- Business
- Industry
- Colleagues
- Professional orgs.
- Online groups

COMMUNITY
- Family/Friends
- Hobbies
- Worship
- Volunteer groups
- Work

The Source of Connection

There are traditional sources for finding network connections:

- School
- Religious organizations
- Clubs (fitness, civic, social)
- Volunteer groups
- Work

These are appropriate places to start, but if all you do is visit with someone on the Sabbath and never engage them beyond that, they are part of your community, but you can't really count them as a network connection. You must activate the relationship to bring them into your network.

If you rely mostly on your work environment for connection, I suggest you broaden your thinking. The problem with relying on your workplace and colleagues to be your main source of network or community is:

- **It's a closed loop.** Unless you have an unusual job, the people you work with are likely from the same company or industry. If you have switched industries, unless you make a conscious effort to maintain the old relationships, they may be part of your community but not part of your network. (A Facebook connection doesn't count unless you are actively connecting about the meaningful work part of your journey.) My suggestion is to be aware of your current network. Consider actively broadening your connections by being interested in others. Look to be helpful to them.
- **You may want to do something completely different in the future.** If you rely on work colleagues to be the core of your network, you will be stuck if you decide (or are forced by circumstances) to try something different. If you include and nurture all kinds of people in your network, you have a much better chance of having a connection who will be helpful to you when you need it.
- **Your work colleagues perceive you in a certain way.** There's usually a hierarchy at work. Who you are and your capabilities are often set by how you're seen, not by your actual skills and aspirations. If you say to your boss, "I know I'm a graphic designer, but I really want to be a writer," they are likely to say, "OK, but what I need you to do is finish your design work." They may be a great boss and fully supportive of your goal, but they are limited in what they can or are willing to do to help you change your path. Similarly, your peers categorize you as that same designer. They may not ever think of you as capable of doing something else. Even if you tell them you want to be a writer, beyond encouragement, it's unclear what they can do.

Always Be Connecting

People say to me, "I need a new job, how do I build a network fast?" The answer is you can't. Networks are built one person at a time. It takes energy and intention to keep your network growing and to keep it strong.

Don't wait until you need a network to build one. The person who could help you get that next job could well be just one connection away in your current network. Unless you are consistently connecting with people, you may never know about or have access to that important secondary connection. Once you need a network to help you, it's too late to build the trust that a network requires.

Building your network of new connections and activating that network is equally important. Don't wait until you need your connections/network to activate them. This means using LinkedIn or another tool to "check in" with people in your network. It's not practical (and in 2020, it may be unhealthy) to have coffee with everyone in your network once or twice a year. That would be great, but it's not feasible. So, how do you keep your network activated? Here are a few ideas:

- Be aware of articles that might interest your connections. If you are in the same field, forward that industry forecast article that you thought captures the essence of the future. (Better yet, write that article!) Even if they have already seen it, they will appreciate your thinking of them, and it will remind them that you are part of their network.
- Jot down notes about your connection's interests or family. I keep mine in the notes in the contacts section of my phone. Maybe your connection loves basketball or honeybees. When you read something of interest or if it's playoff time, let them know you are thinking of them.
- Cross-post. I write a general interest blog, *Hell in the Hallway* (hellinthehallway.net)...when one door closes, another one opens, but it's hell in the hallway. When I post to my blog, I also post it to my LinkedIn network. Even if people don't read my blog, when they see the title and link in their timeline, they (I hope) think of me in a positive light.
- Comment on your connections' posts. If they write a blog or follow a sports team on social media and you also like that blog or team, make that connection.

If you regularly make a conscious effort to check in on people, you will be far better off when you need them. The check-in, however, must be sincere. If you are forcing it, your contact will know (just like you would). The art of keeping a connection warm versus cold is a great skill to cultivate. And do so your way.

And Now...a Story

RORY FINALLY
GETS NETWORKING

☆☆☆☆☆

An introvert, Rory disliked meeting new people. They

had moved several times as a kid and were forced to learn to make friends over and over. You might think that would have made them more comfortable getting to know new people. They could do it but didn't like it. They didn't consider themselves insecure, but meeting new people was a reminder of each move and the discomfort of always being the new kid.

Rory also disliked small talk. They felt it was a requirement for making connections that didn't come from "normal" places like school, work, or organizations for common interests. The thought of going to an event to meet others sounded boring, or worse.

Because they had grown up feeling like an outsider, the idea of making connections for the purposes of helping their career seemed strange. Maybe, they reasoned, they wouldn't have to do it. But then came the day when Rory realized that they wanted to learn more about how they might use their love of travel to earn a living. They looked at their contacts and started asking them if they knew anyone who worked in a travel-related job. They didn't find anyone.

Rory realized that their network was narrow. They had lots of nice people to connect to, but the backgrounds, schools, and work of those connections were limited. Since Rory had never thought of finding work related to their love of travel, they hadn't sought out anyone in that business. They knew other people who enjoyed traveling but they had only had short conversations about it. After talking with a few friends, Rory came to realize that they loved planning the adventure, learning about the new place, and talking to people about what they enjoyed in the location. What they liked least was coming home, unpacking, and organizing the photos. That part was frustrating.

Rory began to realize that people who had a community of colleagues seemed happier. They could talk things over, learn, change, and grow. They decided that even though they were uncomfortable, they wanted what others had: a group of ready-to-help colleagues whom they were also ready to help.

Having coffee with new acquaintances might be OK and in everyone's best interest. Widening the circle of people with whom they were connected became important. They started to prioritize meeting new people and diversifying the kind of people they interacted with.

Trust but Verify

It is not worth expanding your network just for the sake of expansion. Not everyone is worth keeping in your network. By using "trust but verify" as a motto, you may find that you form better relationships and avoid people who aren't in the same mindset of giving to get. In other words, be open to people and expect that they will treat you well. Trust them initially and then do a gut and brain check. Is the relationship in alignment with your values? Are they trying to take advantage of you? Trust but verify means that you don't have to try to change your trusting nature, but you do need to make sure that the person you are giving your precious trust to is actually deserving of it. For example:

- Did they pay attention to what you said, or did they start talking about themselves the minute you stopped talking?
- Do you get a funny feeling in your gut that they don't really see you?
- Do people you trust also trust this person?

If the person appears to be doing right by you, then give them more. If not, slowly back away. This is a good time to pay attention to that little voice inside your head and heart.

If someone abuses your trust (for example, made you feel small or didn't follow through), you may wonder if they should be given a second chance. Certainly, that's a question in the case of an important relationship. Equally important, however, is telling the person truthfully and as kindly as possible how their behavior didn't match your expectation. If you don't tell them, how can they be expected to know? If you have doubts about whether to give a second chance to someone, talk it over with a trusted resource. You don't need advice as much as you need to hear yourself talk about the dilemma out loud.

Tools I Have Used to Grow My Network

Throughout my career, I have come to realize that meeting a wide sampling of people from various backgrounds isn't as easy as I thought. I could naturally meet many other "professionals" who were doing the same kind of work as me, but how could I meet artists, musicians, nonprofit workers, government employees, veterans, people of different religions, races, etc., in a more efficient way than finding them one by one?

I personally like the idea of building community rather than networking. Both accomplish the same goal: broadening and diversifying my worldview. But community building implies we are in it together. That together we are stronger and that we are able do things that in smaller groups, or by ourselves, may not be possible.

I made a conscious effort to reach into other communities and become connected to them. If you are one of the fortunate people who by circumstance or choice already has a broad and diverse network, congratulations! If you happen to be someone who sees opportunity there but are unclear where to start, I hope you start by asking people in your current network how you might work toward this goal.

Here are some tools I used to help me become a better networker and community builder; whether it's going to a party or a professional event, I basically take the same approach.

1. **I attempt to limit the chatter in my head that tries to talk me out of going.** This is a battle that hasn't really changed over the years. If I know I have to go and meet new people, I will invariably try to figure out a way to convince myself that I don't need to go, that I shouldn't go, that going wouldn't do any good. I hope you are laughing as you read that. I am. With the amount of effort I spend attempting to get out of going, I could have gone to the event, met people, and come home. I accept that this is the way I am. I have to trick myself into getting in the car using the following tactics. You probably have your own; maybe mine will help you too.

2. **I "make" myself go—even when I don't feel like it.** There's an old saying: "if nothing changes, nothing changes." Or, "If you always do what you always did, you'll always get what you always got." If I stay in my comfort zone, I'm not going to get the good stuff that life is offering. Worse, I may not change. I didn't want to be same person at forty that I was at twenty. To compete and find meaningful work, I always need new skills and new connections. I know the growing I want to do is going to stem from the people I meet, whose journeys and energies will lift me up and change me forever.

3. **I remind myself that if I don't meet new people face-to-face, then I will miss out on:**

   - Meeting some nice people
   - Making a connection that might change my life
   - Finding a way to help someone with my network that could change their lives

4. **I promise myself that when I have spoken to three new people, I can leave.** You might roll your eyes at a friend who told you they networked but talked only to one person; chances are, though, that you'd congratulate their success at talking with three people. Be that diligent, and that kind, with yourself. Three is a good number—not too many that reaching it feels impossible yet enough that you connect with a diversity of people. Most of the time, once I met three people, I settled into a groove at the event. If I wanted to leave, I could, and half the time, I did.

5. **If I can, I research the attendees and pick out at least one person I want to meet.** Reviewing the list of attendees ahead of time can be useful. The names are not always available, but if they are, check the list for a familiar name or an organization that interests you. I once got a consulting client by identifying someone from an attendance list.

6. **I have stock questions I ask people, so they will talk, and I won't have to.** Everyone asks that same question. "What do you do?" I want to be the unique person in the room. I've learned that when I ask someone what they are passionate about, they start talking and keep talking. I learn so much about them, and I know them in a way that others in the room may not. I've got something interesting to remember them by. I usually draw from this pool of questions:

   - What are you passionate about?
   - What's your favorite body of water?
   - If you had a million dollars, how would you spend it?
   - What's one thing you've always wanted to do but haven't?

There's nothing magical about these questions; think up your own. I tend to stay away from questions about family, origins, age, relationships, children, etc. These questions can make someone uncomfortable, and that would defeat the purpose of meeting them in the first place. There is something magical—but also very real—about what you do after the event. If you are going to build your community, you need to not just meet a ton of people but try to forge a meaningful connection. Do this by being truly interested in other people and then being sure you keep track of them and how you might help them. You could simply send a text saying hi and asking how they are. It's ideal if you know enough that you can ask about something specific. For instance, maybe they play soccer or love reading. Note these details where you keep their contact information.

Make an audit of your current community.

Start by making a list of people that you think might be helpful in your job search. Pick twenty people. (Of course, you will need many more than that, but start with this group.) List each person's name and contact information. Next, list how you know them. You can create categories like:

- Work
- Current
- Previous
- Neighbor
- Church/Temple/Mosque
- School affiliation (college)
- Volunteering
- Friend of friends

If your list consists mostly of people from one or two areas, then you understand how this might be limiting your community. I suggest you take this exercise further and list thirty to forty people. See if the categories expand. See if the number of people in each category expands. Perhaps you're not doing volunteer work or attending church right now. That's OK. The question is, how can you expand the number of people and number of categories from which you are drawing your network?

Learning about what other people do, such as a neighbor you've never really talked to, is a great way to expand your community in an authentic way. Strike up a conversation the next time you run into them; you will likely be surprised to learn the way people earn their living and who they know.

Now, identify one category where you might increase your efforts and set a goal to meet five or ten new people a month. And if that's too much, still do it but set a lower goal.

CHAPTER 9

FINDING A MENTOR

A network is a key part of building flexibility into your work journey. The breadth of your network gives you diverse connections that allow you to help others while they help you. Equally important is gaining support from mentors.

If the network is the breadth, then engaging a mentor is the depth.

There are as many kinds of mentors as there are people. The relationship may be formal or informal, professional or personal. The person may be someone who knows your industry or profession or someone whose general outlook on life you admire. Their assistance may be as narrow as support for a business problem or as broad as guidance along the path of your career.

> *"If the network is the breadth, then engaging a mentor is the depth."*

What Is a Mentor?

A mentor is a person with whom you can talk. The key is finding someone who has the interest and the time to care about you as a person. It is useful for the relationship to be formalized to the extent that both parties agree on a mutually beneficial relationship.

If you think that it's OK to take someone's time and not have any responsibility to the other person, you are wrong. While I'm not suggesting that you need to give anything specific back to the person, I am saying that taking and not showing appreciation or demonstrating awareness of the time and energy you are being given is wrong. Don't do it. If you do, you will defeat the purpose of working to get a mentor in the first place. You will be labeled as ungrateful and may get a negative reputation.

What Makes a Good Mentor/Mentee Relationship?

Several factors make for a good mentor/mentee relationship. The most important ones are:

- **Demonstrating mutual respect**—Pick someone from whom you can learn, whose experience you value. If you pick someone because they have money or are well-connected, you may be disappointed, and so might they. Money and connections are good reasons for network building but lousy reasons for mentorship.
- **Establishing ground rules**—I suggest you (as the mentee) discuss what you are specifically looking for and how often you might want or need to connect. While this may be awkward at the start, it shows maturity on your part and demonstrates respect for the mentor's time. If the person you have asked doesn't recommend setting ground rules, take the initiative. The requests can evolve, but it's a good idea to start with a structure and then grow that structure as your needs change. Depending on the circumstances, I recommend something like a check-in every two weeks. The mentee should always send an agenda ahead of time unless you have agreed otherwise. The mentee also should confirm the appointment the day before. Here's an example: "Hello! Just verifying we're on for tomorrow at 9:00 a.m. I will [call you/send a link, etc.]. Talk to you soon."
- **Maintaining confidentiality**—Both parties must respect the privacy of the other. It's important to spell this out as part of the ground rules. If your mentor mentions something personal or details about their business, you are being trusted to keep that to yourself. If you'd like to share something with someone else that you learned in talking with them, ask your mentor if it would be OK. If you happen to slip and share something that you're not sure you should have, mention it to your mentor immediately. The person will respect you more if you tell them right away and understand your apology way more than if it gets back to them that you shared information that was meant to be kept between you.
- **Having a strong initial session**—Request a time to talk about what you want and, most importantly, why you are asking for their help. This might seem awkward, but if you are unable to articulate why you're asking, you may be disappointed when the person says no.
- **Suggesting a trial period**—Request that the mentoring have a

trial period, so you can both assess the mutual benefit. You might request a check-in after three or four sessions or two to three months or whatever seems appropriate. I require my mentees to mark their calendars for the date of our agreed check-in. It is their responsibility to initiate the check-in. At the appointed date and time, we have a frank discussion about whether the mentorship is working for both of us. This is critical.

- **Saying goodbye**—It's common for people to outgrow a mentor. It doesn't mean anything negative about either of you. It just happens. The more open and frank the communication is in the beginning, the more smoothly any transitions will go. I tell everyone I mentor that they can "fire" me or let me go, anytime. I never take it personally. I lay the groundwork for the ending of the mentorship at the beginning. Most of the time, the relationship lasts for a year or two, and then the person is ready to move on. I've had some mentees for years, others only a few sessions. Either way, the point is mutual benefit. And yes, I have also let mentees go. Disrespect for my time in the form of not confirming appointments, not setting agendas, being unclear about what they want from me, not respecting the time frame we've agreed to, etc., can lead to me terminating the mentorship.

"A good mentor asks questions that expand your way of thinking and helps you see yourself and the way forward in a new light."

- **Focusing on one or two things you want to accomplish**—This may be about problems in your current environment, asking for a raise, or earning a promotion. It may be career related, such as the next job or career changes, or it might be professional development—leadership, skillbuilding, etc. The important thing is to be clear about your goals. They can shift, particularly as the relationship evolves. Things may come up that you hadn't thought of. This is OK and even good. But the responsibility for the relationship falls on you, not the mentor.

- **Sharing experience versus giving advice**—A mentor is not in your life to solve your problems or to fix things. A mentor, in large part, should not give advice. Rather, the person ought to be asking you questions that help you understand the answer for yourself. There is a place for advice, but it's usually best when based on direct experience. I share what I did in a similar circumstance, or I give suggestions. There's a saying about free advice being worth what you pay for it...nothing. A good mentor asks questions that expand your way of thinking and helps you see yourself and the way forward in a new light.

Finding the "Right" Mentor

For me, at different stages in my career, I needed different things. The person I asked to discuss my career with at thirty would not have been very helpful when I was forty and changing careers. That person had never changed careers. I hope you will think of mentors as a series of people who stand by you.

I have been fortunate to have had both men and women as mentors. To me, their gender mattered less than their ability to help me see myself clearly. One mentor helped me change careers. I took a job working for him. He had a reputation for being difficult. I learned that being direct with him was the best way to defuse his aggressive behavior. I learned a lot from him. Another mentor had been my boss. We left our jobs at the same time and started a company together. She was instrumental in changing the course of my career and my life.

There are no specific parameters for identifying the right person, although there are steps you can take to find a mentor who will help improve your chances of success.

Review Mentor Candidates

You may be lucky enough to have someone ask if you need help and offer to be a mentor for you. My experience is that most of us won't get a good mentor by accident. That said, there probably is someone out there who might be a good first mentor or short-term mentor to help you address one or two things that are on your mind. You don't have to have one mentor for life. I suggest you think carefully before diving in. If you are clear about the kind of information or support you want from a mentor, that will help you narrow down who you might ask. I wouldn't ask my math teacher to help me write my essay for an application to a summer journalism program. So be clear about what you are asking for. Think before you ask.

If you're having trouble coming up with candidates, start by thinking of people you admire. What characteristics do they have? Are they bold? Are they a good listener? Are they an expert in something (and do you respect their knowledge)? Do they have experience in something that you need help with? Have they dealt with a similar challenge?

Consider if the person you have in mind is respectful to everyone. Sometimes, we excuse things when it comes to people we admire. We may not see them realistically. If you know someone to be a hothead and you want them to be a mentor, don't be surprised if they are hotheaded with you. Some of us can tolerate that; others can't. Be sure to take their temperament into account.

Don't be afraid that they will say no to your request to be your mentor. They might say no, but then, they might say yes. Even if they say no, the fact that you asked will likely make them think more of you.

If you already know the person you have in mind to ask, then I suggest you ask for a short, informal meeting. Set the meeting for fifteen minutes, no more. Be as clear as you can about how much of their time you are asking for. How much of their time are you asking for? What kinds of topics do you anticipate covering with them? Ask them to think about your request and say that you will follow up with them in a few days. Keeping that first meeting short shows the person you respect their time, as does being clear about what you are asking for.

Also, consider having more than one mentor. You can use them for different purposes. Be clear, however, that each of these relationships takes time and energy to manage. If you have more than one person, you owe each of them your full attention. It is counterproductive to begin a mentoring relationship and then disappoint yourself and the mentor due to lack of focus.

What About Family or Friends?

I don't mentor my family or close friends. If they ask me for my opinion, I'll give it. Otherwise, I keep my opinions to myself. What most family and friends need from me is someone to listen and unconditional support and love.

If you are lucky enough to have a family member who can also serve as a mentor and support, great. If you don't, then you are in the majority. When a family member gets too involved or invested in another person's business, lines can blur, and resentments can flare up. If you are in a family business, you are already aware of this. Some people think that a family business makes it easy. It doesn't. Like all opportunities, there are pluses and minuses. One plus is that if you want a job, one might available. One minus might be that the family needs you to take a job you don't want. Disappointing your family is different than disappointing a stranger.

How I Mentor

I have had the privilege of mentoring both men and women for both business start-up and career purposes. Here's how it works:

- ❦ Some mentees want to talk on a schedule, for example, every other week. Many don't want a "regular" check-in. I am amenable to either.
- ❦ The conversation (in person or by phone or video) is always initiated by the mentee. It is established by them and agreed to by me.
- ❦ I require agendas because without one, the conversation wanders, and I get frustrated. Agendas need to be sent a day or two before the call. If no agenda shows up, the discussion is rescheduled.
- ❦ The mentee is also asked to confirm the meeting at least twelve hours ahead. This lets me know that they are ready for the call.
- ❦ Conversations are about an hour unless we have agreed to a longer time beforehand.
- ❦ I am not a therapist and not a substitute for one. If my mentee finds they are having trouble narrowing down the agenda or staying on topic, then I want them to find additional resources to work through nonproductive thoughts and emotions.

How Do I Ask Someone to Be a Mentor?

Use the following exchange as a guide.

You: Hi. thanks for taking a few minutes to talk with me. I feel a bit awkward about this conversation, so I hope you'll bear with me. [Smile.]
Potential mentor: Of course. You mentioned something about looking for a mentor...I don't know if I have the time, but go ahead.
You: Yes, I'm thinking that I'd like to learn more about [starting a business, being a manager, improving my artwork, etc.]. I have done [X] and [Y] and plan to do more. It occurred to me I could benefit from having someone I could talk with about my progress.
Potential mentor: I'd like to help you, but I don't have a lot of time.
You: I completely understand. I just wanted to get an idea of your interest. Here's what I am looking for. One, the ability to check in once a quarter for thirty minutes to an hour. I will send an agenda

ahead of time. I will bring up a topic or question and briefly tell you what I'm doing and thinking about. If you would be willing to give me your thoughts, I'd be grateful. There would be nothing for you to prepare.

Potential mentor: Well, that sounds like something we could try.

MEANINGFUL | CASE
WORK | STUDY DJ

Where did you grow up?

Nebraska.

What did your parents do for a living?

My mother was a kindergarten teacher, and my father was a manufacturing equipment salesman.

Was your family supportive of your efforts to do meaningful work, or did they think traditional work was better for you?

They always felt traditional work would be better for me.

Tell us about your educational experience.

I graduated high school, went to two years of college, and then dropped out to move from Nebraska to New York and work in a tech start-up.

Are you currently working?

I recently sold my start-up company, so I'm currently working part-time as a freelancer and boiling with ideas!

How do you define meaningful work for yourself?

Meaningful work to me is being able to supply for others who want to create something or be a part of something fun or awesome. My personal values helped me discover that I wanted to create jobs and hire people to work for me so I can help them generate residual income.

What was the single most important step you took to get to this meaningful work?

Putting a pep in your step, learning, plunging right in; even if you don't think you can swim, just giving yourself the shot; if you sink, you'll eventually learn to swim.

Be yourself, love yourself, and work with people who believe in you and want to improve you as a person.

DJ's journey to finding meaningful work:

I was one of those people who never paid attention in class—at least not unless I found something relatable or meaningful to pique my own interests. Some kids would doodle, but I would be writing down ideas for games, thoughts on how to set up an inventory using arrays and loops, and dabbling with programming (designing architecture and logic for logging in to the game).

Ironically, I ended up failing my high school computer class—which is actually pretty funny considering that was the class that interested me the most. As several students who sat behind me watched with amusement, I created little characters in Paint that would hop around the bounds of the window of the application I wrote. The task had been to make a calculator. Needless to say, the teacher was not amused.

Late in high school, the teachers and, well, I guess, everyone started putting pressure on me to figure out where I wanted to go to college and what I wanted to do for a living. I had no idea. I ended up going to a community college for a year and a half because I could not afford to go to college. Later, I saved enough money and took out loans to attend the university I wanted to go to. Meanwhile, I'd dabble in tech, write programs, or even hack things (unofficially continuing my higher education).

I came to find that university was extremely boring; there were so many other people in class, so I felt insignificant. My friends were all set on taking jobs that required specific degrees or certifications or education. I just didn't think I fit in. There weren't really courses like there are today for computer programming or to encourage people to become entrepreneurs and self-sufficient; instead, I was being taught to play the game and pass go—get your paycheck. But I wanted to be the maker of the board game: choose your own destiny.

Then, one day I got a call from some people out in New York offering me a position for building websites. Without hesitating, I went to New York. On the flight out there, I had so many things rushing through my head. I was scared; I knew I couldn't afford living there. I had to make up some story to my parents as to why I'd dropped out of college on a whim. But I made it, started working, and met a small group of people there who let me stay in their families' homes or vacation rentals while I worked.

The most inspirational person I met during that time (right out of college) was a woman from Palermo, Italy. She had pursued her dream and become a prominent model. (Although we eventually ended up moving in together, there was no romantic relationship whatsoever—she treated me as if I were her younger brother, and her brother I became.) She became a great teacher to me and a source of great encouragement; she would always tell me how much of a genius I was. She treated people extremely well and brought me into her family, which also had an impact on me.

Her father was a pizza man in Brooklyn who achieved the American dream; he was extremely hardworking, and in exchange for some pizza from time to time, I would fix his electrical devices (scanner, security system, computers, etc.). He always told me that I'm a good guy and proudly introduced me to other people as if I were his own son. He showed deep compassion to his neighborhood and customers. Through him, I learned that there are so many vultures in the business world, ready to take advantage of the unsuspecting or most vulnerable. Since Alberto didn't speak the best English, people would raise their rates for digital advertisements or for work on his computers. I started to tell him the "actual" price of what someone should charge.

With the encouragement of my "Italian family," peers, friends, and other businesspeople I met, I started my own business. Then, I kept meeting more and more interesting people on my journey of entrepreneurship. I learned all of the positions and expanded my skill set while striving to better myself and give back to others along the way.

What decisions did you make along the way that changed the course of your work life?

- ❦ I had to make the decision to drop out of college, which I knew would not please my mother or father. It was a tough one, knowing I still had student loans to pay.
- ❦ I made the decision to move away from my hometown, which felt like a fresh start in a big city.
- ❦ I shut out "motivational" speeches and how-to books and decided to learn for myself through trial and error.

- I started staying in rather than going out and living the party lifestyle.
- I dropped friends who didn't value me.
- I started to become more generous.
- I decided to start listening to more and more philosophy (timeless information).

What one or two mistakes did you make that taught you a lot?

1. Trusting other people without covering my bottom or learning more about the person's core or goals. I'm convinced you must cover your bottom at all costs. In the mix of things, you just see people as being amazing and that they won't hurt you—so you get all this excitement and pour your passion and hours of work into an idea until you realize the other person thinks you should only get 2 percent and they should get 98 percent, for example.

2. I assumed I had no power or no voice, when I did, and I do. I didn't feel I had power because I felt my accomplishments were small and not worthwhile...and that's simply not true. Make sure you give yourself enough credit and appreciate yourself; be happy with your accomplishments even if they're small or other people don't notice them. With that, I'd like to share the first philosophy quote I've ever held dear, which my mother shared with me and I'll never forget:

    "Forward, as occasion offers. Never look round to see whether any shall note it...Be satisfied with success in even the smallest matter and think that even such a result is no trifle."—Marcus Aurelius

Who are the people or mentors who helped you along the way, and what did you learn from them?

Mentor A: I met this mentor through my "sister." He taught me that if you want to move the earth, you need to use the necessary energy and tools to do so—basically, the importance of "equivalent exchange." He holds a strong belief in Buddhism and shared many things that mattered deeply to him and his decision-making. I call him throughout the year to ask him how he is and how he feels about specific markets. He shares his thoughts freely and always loves good conversation.

Mentor B: This mentor I met while working on a technical project for a client. Words she shared that I won't forget are: "Trust but verify." It's kind of self-explanatory, but I hold that lesson dear. Being such a trusting person, I was letting almost everyone through. The perspective that in even the stickiest of situations, I have an abundance of choices is huge. I ended up sharing this concept with a few people who seek advice from me, and they've found that it has given them power and strength. I also learned that it's always OK to ask for help. This has helped me to feel more comfortable even talking to other mentor-like figures in my life. Finally, I learned to just "listen" more to people and that this alone can open many doors. Through all of the knowledge I've gained from this mentor and others, I am more comfortable in my decisions, and while I still face battles, I feel more equipped going forward.

Mentor C: This mentor is extremely generous, gracious, and appreciative. He taught me that when the seed is good, to sow it, and it will one day feed me. He had a major impact on my life by getting me a ticket to attend an educational networking event and introducing me to ideas of Robert Kiyosaki (and playing the physical board game Cash Flow). In that educational course, I was able to listen to and learn from people such as Jack Welch, Randi Zuckerberg, Hugh Hilton, and Al Pacino for six hours in the day. My hand was sore from taking so many notes. Many of those people talked about how to build something that can scale or grow.

Find a mentor.
1. Brainstorm a list of things a mentor might be useful for on your journey. Right now, don't think about who, just concentrate on what. Do you feel stuck? Write about that. What has happened or is happening in your job or job history? What is going well? What isn't? What experiences would help you grow?
2. Make a list of at least five people you admire. Broaden your thinking to people you respect. Right now, you're not thinking about asking anyone—you are simply working to identify people and types of people who might work as mentors. (If they are in your family, that's OK, but if the only people on your list are family members, that may limit the kind of mentor you get.) If you've worked on your network, glance at that list with a new set of eyes. Who on the list do you trust, admire, and respect? What kind of person are they? What do they do for a living? What qualities about them stand out to you?
3. Role-play with a friend, asking someone to be your mentor. Be sure to be clear about what you are asking for. What's in it for the mentor? The clearer you are about all of this, the better your chances are of getting a yes to your request.
4. Think about times when you were coached, maybe in sports or in a school subject or club. Be honest: How coachable were you? Did you enjoy having guidance, or did you resent it? We all have experiences with coaches, "good" and "bad." It's how we respond to each that matters. This mini self-assessment is a worthwhile exercise whether you ever ask for a mentor or not. If you can't think of any experience you've had with a coach, then it's time to create an opportunity. Start small. Ask someone for guidance on one topic and see how it goes.

CHAPTER 10

THE PULL OF ENTREPRENEURSHIP AND INDEPENDENT WORK

Today, the most effective career counseling encourages entrepreneurial and independent work options. The jobs that many millennials will have twenty years from now aren't even on the radar of "jobs to apply for" today. If you look online for "jobs that didn't exist twenty years ago," here are some of the jobs that come up:

- App developer
- Social media manager
- Virtual assistant
- Podcast manager
- Lyft driver
- Cloud architect

Five years from now, there will likely be many more jobs in the following fields, where only some jobs exist today:

- Artificial intelligence
- 3D printing
- Robotics
- Drone technology
- Sustainability
- Cannabis

These fields will influence big industries like:

- Technology
- Health care

- Media
- Hospitality
- Consumer products and services
- Energy

It takes imagination to predict where the jobs will be. One thing is certain: jobs will change, and the more flexible and prepared we are, the better.

Many of these jobs need technical people, but companies will also need accountants and human resources, marketing, and finance professionals, etc. If you are have even passing experience in one of the emerging areas, you will have an advantage over those who "played it safe." How are we supposed to think about what job we want or what skills to develop when the job doesn't even exist yet?

Whether you are creating a new start-up, driving for Uber, or freelancing as a graphic designer, you are part of a growing percentage of the workforce who is doing independent work. There are many names for this:

- Freelancer
- Independent contractor
- Independent consultant
- Gig worker
- 1099 employee

You are likely aware of other classifications of independent work to add to this list. For our purposes, I'm going to talk about two categories: entrepreneurship and independent work. As you think about future meaningful work, understanding and considering the world of entrepreneurship and independent work become important. I hope this chapter provides you with food for thought.

What Is Entrepreneurship?

Entrepreneurs start new endeavors. Employees of a start-up are not in this category because, while they may be taking a risk and learning valuable skills, they are employees and get a paycheck. However, if someone works as an independent contractor for a start-up, that person falls into this group of people.

As you drive around your town or city, start to notice all the small businesses. They are everywhere—diners, laundromats, hair salons, convenience stores, etc. Each of these was established by someone who had a desire to be their own boss. Whether they inherited, bought, or set up the business from scratch, an entrepreneur is responsible for every aspect of the business, including selling, buying, hiring, legal, financial, and marketing. They have taken on financial risks in the hopes of satisfying a customer need for a profit.

Entrepreneurial ventures often have employees who help build the system that will generate revenue and sustain the business for the future. One can work in and learn about setting up and growing a business without being the business owner. Entrepreneurial ventures need workers who are willing to share the risks:

- Employment stability—working at a start-up or in a small business may be riskier than a larger organization
- Money—accepting a lower wage or other financial benefits in order to help a new company grow

People who work in these emerging businesses trade stability and financial reward for a chance to be part of a new and growing venture.

What Is Independent Work?

There are legal reasons why there so many divisions in employment "status." There are tax and regulatory implications for each status. Companies with employees have financial and statutory requirements to those employees. Companies like Postmates, Lyft, Grubhub, and hundreds of others, classify and pay workers as independent to avoid those requirements. There are arguments on both sides of the employment coin as to whether this categorization is fair to workers. I'm not going into that here.

Independent workers make their own decisions about how, when, and where they work (and sometimes for how much). They are hired by clients to fulfill a specific task or project. They are self-employed and can work any number of hours per week. Assignments range from graphic design or photography to coding projects and consulting assignments. They work for themselves and, many times, by themselves.

Independent workers are not protected by federal and state laws in the same way employees are. There is no minimum wage, health insurance, retirement, or civil rights protections. On the positive side, these workers control their schedule and work on the projects they choose. In response to this expanding workforce, the Freelancers Union (freelancersunion.org) was founded to help address issues important to this group of workers.

The Growth of Independent Work

About 57 million people (36 percent of US workforce)[20] are now employed as independent workers. Drivers and delivery services are just two categories of these workers. Prior to the growth of the internet (late 1990s), the process of finding a profession or career had a typical path for those privileged enough to be the right gender, ethnicity, age, etc. Working independently wasn't even on the radar for most workers. Money and benefits far outweighed any perceived benefits of working for yourself. Today, setting up a business, working remotely, finding customers, earning a living all became reasonable for an individual to accomplish.

Independent work can serve as a means to:

- Build new skills
- Learn about yourself
- Broaden your network
- Try out new environments
- Test your fitness for risk-taking

Entrepreneurs and Independents: Similarities

Independent workers are entrepreneurs in that they set up a business and take the financial risk. But not all entrepreneurs derive their income from independent sources. For some, their start-up is a side gig, but both choose what hours they work, and both are responsible for running their own business (paying taxes, getting health insurance, etc.).

Entrepreneurs and Independents: Differences

Independents get paid when they work. Entrepreneurs work to satisfy a customers' needs. They may work many hours for no pay in hopes of setting up a system to make money. One other important difference—if the freelancer quits, their business doesn't exist anymore. If the entrepreneur moves on, the business may or may not continue, depending on how solid its foundation is and who is in place to keep the doors open.

Independent Work: The Good, the Bad, and the Downright Ugly

The Good: Freedom!

Rewards in the form of:

- Choosing working hours and what work to do
- Doing work that feels useful and meaningful
- Creating a thriving work culture
- Enjoying a potential financial upside
- Earning all the rewards for your hard work, not sharing with a company
- Learning, being creative, and using a lot of skills
- Experiencing an ever-changing and growing environment

The Bad: Increased Risk

- Financial insecurity—can't make enough money, trouble collecting money from clients
- Mental anguish—unable to motivate yourself to get the work done
- Loss of self-esteem—can't adjust to not being as successful as before
- Long hours—there's a reason they call it a grind
- Personal relationship strain—hard on family and friends who do not understand the drive it takes to make a new venture work

The Ugly: Uncertainty

On paper, the good and the bad things seem manageable. But the truth is that independent work is not for sissies. Here's one example of how things can go wrong, despite our best planning.

We say to ourselves, "I have savings; I can wait out the slow months." And that's 100 percent true. What we can't anticipate is the feeling of uncertainty. That we're never sure when unforeseen expenses will be needed or when cashflow might go from positive to negative. One of the things most entrepreneurs don't know or think about is how hard it can be to collect money owed by clients. Even when we get a client and do the work, collecting the money can be delayed or, in the worst cases, impossible to collect.

I don't say all this to scare you but to make you aware that while the idea of being able to work independently may seem desirable, it has its pitfalls. Being your own boss, setting your own hours, etc., all seem a perfect solution to the "I hate my boss" dilemma. The reality is, most of us have no idea what it takes to start and run a business. We are unprepared for the financial, psychological, and personal roller coaster that comes with independence. Some of us are temperamentally unsuited to the insecurity. For most of us, there's only one way to find out. Try it.

The Benefits of Entrepreneurship

Entrepreneurs learn and practice skills that are valuable regardless of whether you work for yourself or someone else. Rapid decision-making, flexible thinking, risk-taking, opportunity evaluation, and prototyping are just a few examples. The reasons I wholeheartedly support entrepreneurial training for anyone are:

- Learning is hands-on and practical.
- Many of the skills are transferable.
- It's fun. Being part of something new is exciting and building something from the ground up is rewarding.

Independent work is one way to get acquainted with these skills and gain the benefits without all the risk involved in a start-up.

What Does the Entrepreneur Do?

Before I had my business, I thought I'd spend most of my time doing the work that I knew I could do. I was a consultant. I had done that work as an employee for a long time. I knew how to do it. What I was underprepared for were two other important aspects of having a business. I thought I would just have to do the work. What I didn't realize was that I would also need to do the following:

1. Run the business. Setting up a business is work. Deciding on the legal entity, learning about regulatory and financial requirements, hiring employees, taking care of the business accounts, managing the "office" (Where's the stapler? How come the printer isn't working? What happened to my Wi-Fi?)—all that is just plain work. When I was employed, my company took care of all that. Now it was all on me.

2. Grow the business. While I hoped that new clients would find me—and luckily, I had a background in sales and marketing—I

had never marketed myself or written a proposal to a client to sell them my services. I understood in principle what I needed to do, but selling myself was uncharted territory.

Every business needs to keep one eye on growth. Is it growing? Is it growing quickly enough? Or too quickly? How will the company build connections to both customers and potential partnerships? The hard part is identifying appropriate ways for the growth to occur and then finding a way to facilitate that.

A Word about Risk-Taking and Risk Aversion

Some of us, by virtue of temperament or upbringing, feel more comfortable taking risks. For others, risk aversion is standard operating procedure. It is useful to understand our comfort with taking risk. There are online assessments you can use for this purpose. I would argue, however, that taking those tests prior to taking an entrepreneurial plunge may be self-defeating, and here's why.

Starting a company is like trying a new food. More complex but the metaphor is still valid. Some people are very adventurous in trying new foods; some are not. But that doesn't mean that someone (except those with health conditions) can't try new foods. The question isn't yes or no—it's...what new foods could I try that would fit with who I am? If I have eaten spicy foods from childhood, then trying a new spicy food probably wouldn't be much of a

> "Starting a company is like trying a new food...Some people are very adventurous in trying new foods; some are not. But that doesn't mean that someone...can't try new foods. The question isn't yes or no—it's... what new foods could I try that would fit with who I am?... The same goes for independent work."

stretch. But if I've never tried spicy food, probably dumping sriracha all over my food isn't a good idea. We can try something that maybe we thought we'd wouldn't like, but that doesn't mean we have to like it or eat it for the rest of lives. We experiment with food and cuisines and learn what tastes good to us. The same goes for independent work. Look for an experiment to run that seems appropriate for your level of comfort in risk-taking.

What I Have Learned from Entrepreneurs

Having worked as a mentor with hundreds of entrepreneurs over the years, I've found that I learned as much, if not more, from each of them as they learned from me. I felt fortunate to be trusted by such talented people. Here are a few things I witnessed in them.

- ❧ **Passion:** Every person reinforced for me the power and importance of passion. Each is driven by their own vision and experience. If you are going to have a start-up, you need to love the core subject. You are going to spend a lot of time thinking about and working on this idea. Be sure you have the passion to sustain you.
- ❧ **Plug-in:** They meet challenges with energy and take each as an opportunity to reinvest.
- ❧ **Pivot:** Equally as powerful is their ability to work hard and to follow where their start-up journey takes them. They seem to gain strength from being able to follow a new path.
- ❧ **Pursue:** Whether their first idea was successful or not (usually not), they take everything they learn from each venture and use it to fuel a new idea.

One thing about hanging around entrepreneurs is that everyone is excited. On any given day they might feel discouraged, but in general, the pride and passion they feel for their venture is contagious. This is in sharp contrast to employees who dislike their jobs and are counting the days until they can change jobs to something more rewarding.

MEANINGFUL CASE
WORK STUDY

Where did you grow up?

I grew up in Wisconsin, in a small university city.

What did your parents do for a living?

My dad was a credit union loan officer, and my mom was an administrative assistant at the university.

Was your family supportive of your efforts to do meaningful work, or did they think traditional work was better for you?

I was blessed to have parents who supported whatever career path I chose, so long as it made me happy. Like most parents, they would have preferred if I'd stayed close to home and pursued a long-term "stable" job, but they knew early on that was not likely to happen (I was much too independent and filled with wanderlust!). While in college, I got involved in the Campus Activities Board (CAB), which brought live music to campus. I also worked at a local music venue, solidifying my (then) dream of working in the music industry. After I graduated college, my parents helped me move to Nashville, Tennessee (where I didn't yet have a job!).

Throughout my life, however, I was always writing stories and poems and entering writing contests. As a child, I told everyone I wanted to be a writer when I grew up. My parents were extremely supportive of that dream as well, although I set it aside as I grew older, not believing it to be lucrative.

Tell us about your educational background.

I have a bachelor's degree in communication studies with a minor in German. What I gained from college was much less about academic study and much more about the passion I had for music and the knowledge and network I gained from my extracurricular activities.

After studying in Vienna, Austria, one summer, I felt my wanderlust explode as I learned there were so many incredible people to meet and places to see if I just looked for them. I maintained a heavy course load each semester in order to graduate in three and a half years; I was more than ready to get out of my hometown and explore the rest of the world.

How do you define meaningful work for yourself?

To me, meaningful work is work that makes you feel alive. We feel alive when we are doing the work we are "meant" to do! As a result, it is likely to contribute to the common good in some way—whether we realize it or not.

R's journey to finding meaningful work:

I am blessed to have found work that I love. I have been self-employed since 2014, working full-time as a ghostwriter and editor for my company. Most days, it doesn't even feel like work. My journey to get here, however, was full of twists and turns.

Working in the music industry was meaningful to me because I always feel so alive when I listen to music I love, but it's a hard industry to break into. I applied at countless record labels and booking agencies before landing a (very-low-paid) internship with a booking agency representing the college circuit. I lasted only a few months; I essentially felt like a telemarketer. I realized I didn't want to sit behind a desk; I wanted to be where the action was.

I got another (very-low-paid) job working as an usher at the Ryman Auditorium in Nashville. I even supplemented that job working as a security guard at local concerts and festivals. These jobs barely paid the bills, but the job at the Ryman remains one of the most meaningful jobs of my life. I made incredible friends who all shared my passion for music, and I got to see some of the most amazing artists perform.

After working for minimum wage, I'd accrued significant debt (in addition to my college debt), so I knew I needed to get a "real" full-time job. I figured if I had to sit behind a desk, it might as well be one that "mattered." I landed a job at Big Brothers Big Sisters, and although I loved the organization, clocking in, doing paperwork, and working in an office was soul-sucking. After two years, I needed a change. A big one.

I sold what didn't fit in my car, parked my car at my parents' house, and bought a one-way ticket to Argentina. I would spend six months there over the next two years. In between two trips, I moved to Portland, Oregon. I had very little money and no job, but the city seemed to attract seekers, like me. Over the next several years, I changed jobs more often than some people change clothes. I never again took a full-time job because I knew it would take all my creative energy. I worked as a teacher, cashier, dog walker, and more. Eventually I realized I would never be happy working for someone else.

I then started a Spanish language/English as a Second Language (ESL) business. At first, it was great. I learned a lot about operating a small business; it was all so new and exciting. Two years later, the business was successful, but I didn't feel mentally stimulated anymore. I sold my ownership and started a new business—an ecofriendly gift basket company for pet lovers! That was fun too... until I realized that staying in one place (with all that inventory!) didn't satisfy my love of travel. That business had to go.

This is when I started my current business. First, I wrote a memoir, a story I felt I needed to tell. That experience changed my life. While I didn't make much money with that book, I learned many valuable lessons. One is that I am not attached to having my name on a book. Ghostwriting was a clear path for me. I wanted to help other people tell their stories, and not just any stories—meaningful stories, stories that change lives. My clients are special in that they see the world through a lens of gratitude and believe that everyone's life has a higher purpose and that their book is not about them—it's about the people it touches.

This work never feels dull. I don't have to "recover" from the workday, week, or year because the work itself is rejuvenating. I can work from the beach, another country, or the couch with my cat. Each book project feels like a new job, so I'm continuously learning and growing. I don't have to please a boss—only my clients. I don't have to clock in at a certain time; I can stay up late and sleep in.

Self-employment isn't for everyone. Some people like structure and companionship and the perceived stability of working for someone else. I work hard, wear many hats, and sometimes worry whether I'll have enough money to pay the bills next month. But I'm willing to trade money for meaning any day. The money always seems to show up when I need it.

Any other thoughts about finding meaningful work?

Listen to that voice that spoke up when you were a child. Chances are, you knew more about yourself then than you do now.

Also, if you are pursuing self-employment, don't be afraid to make a financial investment in training and networking—these have paid off in spades for me.

Consider being your own boss.

1. Most of us have an idea for a business. Whether we ever pursue that idea or not, there is value in creating a list of business ideas and then researching one or two to understand what it takes to learn how to evaluate an idea. When you get an idea for business, jot it down. I like to keep my business ideas in one file. I never know when an idea might morph into something else, as technology, time, or who I know changes. For instance, until we had mobile phones, there was no need for apps. Once the phone was ubiquitous, apps by the thousands were needed and invented. You might sit down with a friend and brainstorm. Think about problems you or your loved ones face every day and how you might solve them.

2. From that list, pick one business idea to research. I suggest starting by mapping out what the customers' needs are. One of the most common problems I notice in the start-up world is falling in love with an idea and neglecting to understand the customer. Mapping gets us away from "What do I have to do to make this work?" and gets us to focus on "Does my customer need this, and what requirements does the customer have?" While harder, starting with the customer is one of the keys to a successful business.

3. Identify one or two skills that you think would help you on an independent work journey. Do you currently have a lack of experience in financials, for example? Find places and people with whom you can start to learn. Make a list of local or web-based places where you might contribute. It may be volunteer, internship, or paid. As you make and review the list for a good place to start, be sure to think about your strengths, values, and goals. Assess opportunities based on what and from whom you want to learn. Do this, but also allow for serendipity. Trust your gut. It will guide you.

CHAPTER 11

BOSS SHOPPING

O nce upon a job, I had a great boss. She was the first female boss I'd ever had, and she taught me a great deal about being a good manager. She taught me to listen and stay focused on an objective. She showed me how to help a team reach difficult goals and how to ask for help. She told me when I was doing something wrong and praised me when I deserved it.

The first time I met her, she asked me a question that no boss had ever asked me. "What would you like to be doing, and where do you think you can make a difference?" I was blown away by the question and grateful that I had a good answer! If your boss asked you that question, what would you say?

Working for her made me realize how important a boss is. Even though no one ever told me that I could go shopping for a boss, I figured out from that experience that I wanted a boss who would:

- teach me things and help me grow,
- care enough to teach me how to be responsible for my own professional development,
- show me how to be an effective manager and leader, and
- be a role model for how to treat others.

After that, I vowed never to work for someone I didn't respect or believe I could learn from. I became a boss shopper.

Boss shopping is not shopping like a boss; it's shopping for a boss, rather than for a job. This means deliberately seeking a person to work for rather than a job to do.

This might sound strange. Maybe you're wondering, "What if I get the boss I want and hate the job?" My experience is that jobs often turn out to be different than what was expected. The way I look at it, if I am going to work for someone I respect and who respects me, at least I have a fighting chance of making the best of the situation.

Boss shopping is different from job shopping in that we look for and at people, not job titles. This means starting from the mindset of

"Who would I learn from?" This shift gives us an opportunity to shine a whole new light on work and jobs. We get out of the rut of profession, industry, and job title and consider how we spend our precious time and energy.

Unconventional thinking is useful to help us consider alternatives on our journey. Boss shopping is one of those nontraditional paths. As we travel the work road, we will intuitively know who supports us and who doesn't.

As we identify people who see and hear us, we grow more comfortable expressing ourselves. If we have to hide most of who or what we are, we expose ourselves to forces that may work to undermine us. But as we accept responsibility for our own career, contentment, and success (meaningful work), we learn to trust ourselves and our judgment. We reward our boss for seeing us and supporting us by doing our best work. We get the support of someone who will help us grow, change, and learn.

Learn Something from Every Boss

Boss shopping may take a little getting used to. Begin now by thinking about your current boss. Regardless of whether your current work is meaningful, think about the following:

- What motivates them?
- What is their managerial style?[21]
- How do they interact with other employees? Do they behave differently with different people?
- Who gets rewarded with attention, assignments, etc.?

If we believe they have something to teach us, we can learn something from each of them. That may be how not to behave. This can be frustrating, but it is usually valuable. Take each boss as they come and ask, what is this person teaching me? Even if the lesson is what not to do.

If your boss is coaching you on what you need to improve on, but they share the information in a way that doesn't sit well with you, you may need to learn to live with their style. Work on receiving the information with a more open mind.

Why Bosses Are So Important

You work for a person, not a company. The person who authorizes your paycheck is the person who most influences your job. This may not seem true, especially in larger organizations. For the most part, however, your boss influences your pay, hours, opportunities, and your future in the organization.

If you doubt this, try going around your boss. Most environments have hierarchies. That chain-of-command mentality is deeply embedded in the culture, and it doesn't appreciate a person who doesn't understand "how things work around here." If you work in a small place or in a more democratic, less egocentric place, it may be better. I guarantee that there are still norms.

People in power do not easily hand over control.

No matter where you work, be aware that you work for a person—your boss. Yes, your paycheck comes from an organization,

> "Boss shopping is not shopping like a boss; it's shopping for a boss, rather than for a job. This means deliberately seeking a person to work for rather than a job to do."

but your near-term future depends on the person who can say yes or no to your raise, promotion, or opportunities. If you have more than one boss, which happens frequently, take the opportunity to learn from each.

And Now...a Story
DREW FINDS A NEW JOB...
BY FIRST SHOPPING FOR A BOSS

☆☆☆☆☆

Drew went to college for accounting. They liked accounting but were growing tired of the push and pull of politics at their company. Certain clients (that is, large companies) were given great service. Small clients, who represented an increasing part of the company's growth, were courted by the best salespeople and given incentives to use Drew's company's services. However, when it came to supporting these smaller clients, Drew was told to spend the minimal amount of time with them. This concerned Drew because they were being given more and more small clients. These companies were beginning to rely on Drew to answer important tax and financial questions. To answer these questions, they needed time to look for solutions.

Drew approached their boss and explained their frustration. The boss listened to Drew but told them that this is "the way it is." Drew would just have to "figure it out." It was clear to Drew that a serious mistake was inevitable. It was only a matter of time before they would give an incorrect answer that would trigger a negative experience for one of their clients.

Although Drew was always looking for opportunities, it was clear that, at this time, there wasn't a job to move into inside the company. Drew decided to make a list of people, both inside and outside the company, whom they admired. Drew kept an open mind as they wrote this list. They would not eliminate someone simply because their job or title or organization didn't seem like an appropriate fit for Drew's longer-term career goals. Drew had faith that finding a potential boss would, at least, lead to a list of interesting people.

Drew's list had these individuals:

- ★ The director of operations for a large nonprofit that provided services to the blind and visually impaired
- ★ A sales manager who worked in financial services
- ★ Someone who ran three bakeries around Drew's city
- ★ A friend who worked in a family business

None of these individual jobs or workplaces were on Drew's "career path." Drew struggled to think how they would explain a job move to any of these organizations. As they weighed each, they began to focus less on their career path and more on the person they might work for. In their networking, Drew had a chance to talk with three of the four people on the list. Some they met in person; some they spoke with on the phone. Each was generous with their time. One of them, however, stood out over the others, and Drew knew they would learn a lot working for this individual. Drew liked how this person:

- ★ spoke about their colleagues and the work they did together,
- ★ had passion for the business, and
- ★ had experience in three different industries, not just the one they were currently in.

Drew had no idea what kind of work they might do for a chain of bakeries, but they thought it would be worthwhile to approach this person. Within three months, Drew had a job doing part-time accounting and part-time operations management for one of the bakeries. Had Drew kept looking for an accounting job, they never would have found this opportunity. Not long into their new job, Drew realized how valuable this operations experience would be when and if they returned to full-time accounting work.

Would Drew have been happy working for any of these people? Maybe. It's great to keep a list of people who would make good bosses. You never know—shopping for a boss may be the ideal way to open doors in your journey for meaningful work.

Things to Ponder While Boss Shopping

⊕ **No one wants to work for a jerk.** A bad boss may be stupid, ignorant, or unethical. Is one worse that the other? Who cares? A boss who is disrespectful, micromanaging, blankety-blank (fill in your own words) needs to be avoided. However, if only one person tells you someone is difficult, it may be the person, not the boss, who's difficult. Get multiple perspectives on the boss candidate.

⊕ **What kind of boss fits your style best?** What kind of environment helps you be the most productive? Pay attention to the kind of feedback, tasks, and approaches that work best for you. The "wrong" boss takes a lot of energy to manage—energy that could better serve productivity.

⊕ **How open is the boss?** Are they set in their ways or open to new ways of getting things done? Bosses who are flexible help broaden your experiences.

⊕ **What makes a "good" boss for you?** One way to think about this is, what makes a good teacher? For some, a good teacher is tough; they expect a lot and give hard tests. That style might be useful to some people but maybe not to you. The more we understand what works for us, the more likely we are to be productive under the guidance of that type of leader. There are as many kinds of bosses as there are people.

⊕ **A good boss teaches you how to be a good employee.** This may be counterintuitive. I mean, what is a good employee? Showing up on time? Getting your work done? OK. But it also means, for instance, learning how the boss wants to be kept up-to-date on project work. Some bosses will tell you straight out what they want: *Give me a weekly report in writing.* Or, *Come to me with a problem and a potential solution, not just a problem.*

This may be a tough kind of boss for some. If there's no give and take, no interaction, no chance to learn by talking, you might think this is a negative. If your boss is like this and you're unable to adjust, then it may be time to start looking for a new gig. If, however, your new boss gives you great opportunities but doesn't want to interact, maybe you can adjust to the lack of interaction in exchange for the chance to have these opportunities. Since your boss is your ticket to increases in pay and opportunities for advancement, it's in your best interest to find a way to communicate. Be proactive in asking what kinds of options work best for them. Propose different scenarios for communication and getting feedback that might be mutually beneficial.

Red Flags When Boss Shopping

It's worthwhile to consider "red flags" when boss shopping. Trusting one's gut is a learned skill. If you were raised in an emotionally life-affirming environment, you may not need help. But some of us can use ideas and support when considering taking this approach to finding meaningful work. Here are a few red flags to watch out for:

- **Behaving unprofessionally**—A boss may try to take advantage of their position. There is no way to know ahead of time whether this is going to happen, but if it does, walk away. For example, if someone asks you out or makes comments that make you uncomfortable, trust yourself. Don't make excuses for their inappropriate behavior. I recommend not dating people who might be your mentors or bosses, no matter how attractive or interesting the person is. These are delicate relationships, and they need trust. Crossing the line into personal relationships is likely to create difficult and complicated problems, no matter how innocently the relationship may start. If someone asks you to join them for dinner or drinks to "discuss it further," please think carefully. Coffee and lunch are better choices. If you find yourself attracted to a person you are considering as a potential boss, stop and take at least two weeks before you have any contact with the person again. These things are easy to get into and hard to get out of.

- **The control freak**—These people may not be as easy to spot as you might think. When you don't work for them, they often appear generous and even tempered. But when you work for them, they become micromanagers. If you deal well with this management style, then you're OK. If you are a self-starter who prefers autonomy, beware. If you have any doubt, try to find someone who worked for them previously. Ask general questions about working for this person. Trust your gut.

- **The self-server**—Some people who seem generous actually are focused on their own personal career progress. These people can be charming, but when you know their career story, you understand there has been significant advancement. In their wake may be employees who gave them their ideas and hard work—or had their efforts taken without compensation. When you ask them about the people they have mentored or how their employees have progressed, their answers become vague. Don't be fooled. Watch their body language. If they look down or begin to fidget, notice it.
- **Poor communication skills**—A good boss knows how and when to communicate. Employees need enough information to do the job, but of course, there are times when a boss can't share everything. What I'm talking about here is when you work for someone who habitually leaves you in the dark or puts you in a position where better communication on their part would have saved a lot of time and trouble. This problem may take one of the following forms:
  - Black hole—Information goes in but rarely comes out. This boss isn't a bad person; they just aren't attuned to the need to share information with their employees. This kind of boss may be hard to work for, but it's likely that everyone around them knows how they are.
  - Information hoarder—This type of person believes that information is power and wants to keep information so that they "win." This is a bad kind of boss to work for. They often have "an in order for me to win, you have to lose" mentality. Not good.
  - Limited skills—This kind of boss, because of either personality or experience, doesn't know how important communication is in order to get the job done. When combined with incompetence, this boss is a nightmare.
- **Unethical**—This red flag may take time to reveal itself. Bosses who want to get ahead at any cost use unethical behavior as one of their tools. They are often good at hiding their motives and have allies who help them get ahead. Once you sense or have information confirming that the person you work for or are interviewing with lacks scruples, it is time to move on.

There are likely many other red flags to look out for. Trust your gut.

If you sit with your potential boss and have a funny feeling about the person, trust it. Your "spidey sense" about people is your best guide.

And Now...a Story

ALEX EVALUATES A BOSS

Alex had been looking for a new job for three months. They were currently working as a restaurant server and writing part-time for an aquaculture ezine. Alex had a long-time interest in sustainability that led them to work at a tilapia fish farm while in high school and then at a similar gig in college. Their server job was helping to pay down the student loans but was draining Alex of any creative energy. Alex had an interview at a climate change nonprofit. The organization seemed well-funded, and the information on the website sounded like it lined up with Alex's beliefs. Here's Alex:

"The job sounded great. I wanted to work in sustainability, but more importantly, I wanted to work on solutions to feeding the people of our changing planet. I liked the people I met. I thought I asked good questions. I thought that since the people were nice and the mission matched mine, it would work out. In my current job, I basically have to do what I'm told. I wanted a challenge that would let me learn new skills and work toward solutions. I even asked questions about how the project work got done. Everything was lining up.

"When I got there, it turned out that grant funding drove all the decisions about what work got done. My boss didn't value my time or my opinion. It was all about the grant. I was just a pair of hands. I felt like I made a huge mistake leaving my server job where I made good money for a job I now hate."

In talking to Alex about their job research, I asked about their questions during the interview. The answer was "I didn't ask many specific questions about what work I would be doing. I just thought from the way I felt in the interview that my boss would respect my opinion. It's worse than being a server."

I asked Alex about other job interviews and bosses they'd had. Alex told me that the worst boss they'd ever had (besides an embezzler!) was a micromanager. Alex got excellent performance reviews, but this boss drove them crazy. Alex wondered what they could have done to prevent working for this type of person again. Looking back on the interview, Alex realized that the signs were there. Not just in the excruciatingly neat desk and office but in the future boss's attitude.

When Alex asked their future nonprofit boss how much autonomy they gave the team, the boss's answer was "Oh, a lot." But thinking back, Alex remembered that they immediately looked down and quickly changed the subject. Alex had a follow-up question but never asked it and thought it was awkward to come back to it. Upon reflection, Alex realized that it was their responsibility to make sure, in the future, that they paid a lot of attention to not just what the person said but what their body language gave away. They also learned to not be so eager for any job that they ignored their own needs.

Imagine an ideal boss.

1. Think about five people who have had authority over you. It may help to think of teachers or professors whose styles you liked and disliked. You may include your parents if you want, but if you can, think of five people other than family members, unless you also work for them. Write down three positive qualities about each and three negatives. If you need help thinking about ways to evaluate these people, search for information on what makes a good boss versus a bad boss and use any helpful criteria listed. The goal here is not so much to criticize the person but rather to review your own criteria for dealing with a boss. You are looking for a pattern of what works for you.

2. Reference your values list from chapter five. If you haven't read that chapter yet, write down a few values that you think are important to you. As you think about this list, focus on factors that affect your work. As you compare the lists, think about what is most important to you and then formulate questions that might help you discover whether you are compatible with the potential boss.

3. Practice paying attention to people's body language. Being able to "read" people comes naturally to some. For the rest of us, it takes practice.

4. Think about someone you know well. Notice a time when they said one thing, but you know they meant something else. How did you know that? Was it the tone of their voice? The way their body slumped a little? Understanding how body language helps us learn when someone is being open or closed is a good skill to have. Check out Amy Cuddy (amycuddy.com) for more information on the importance of body language in the workplace. Amy's TED Talk[22] on how body language may shape who you are is great place to start.

CHAPTER 12

WHERE DO YOU FIT IN?

O ne day while walking my dog with a young friend, I asked them about their roadblocks to finding work they enjoy. They said finding a "job" was relatively easy, but finding a workplace where it felt like they fit was hard. They were continually disappointed by the work environment, more than with the job itself. When I asked them to explain further, they said the main problem was finding a workplace where they could contribute, learn, and feel valued.

I interviewed several younger people to understand their main complaint about work. Their complaints related to:

☙ Inclusion
☙ Opportunities to receive honest feedback
☙ Opportunities to grow
☙ Clear paths to increased responsibility

This shared experience of struggling to find a workplace where one fits is a relatively new part of the job search process. It is especially compelling for millennials and Gen Z because those of you in these groups are pursuing a career path at a time of rapid change.

For baby boomers, frequently changing jobs was a sign that an employee was unstable. The pressure to stay in a job or at a company drove many boomer choices. Seldom did a worker decide to switch companies on a whim. The following factors drove many boomer job choices:

☙ Stability of the employer
☙ Retaining a job
☙ Loyalty
☙ Compliance
☙ Gratitude for their job
☙ Respect for authority

Today, changing jobs is normal. The pressure to remain in a job or in a certain field is lessened by the number of opportunities available and the pace of change. In today's environment, broadening skills and experiences is necessary for survival.

There's no guarantee that any job, boss, organization, etc., will be what we need. But we can give ourselves a fighting chance at working somewhere that supports us for who we are. It's important that our workplace not take us off our path of self-compassion and growth. Staying the course, however, requires work, discipline, and attention.

Improve Your Chances

When you say you do or don't "fit in" at work, you are likely speaking about feeling comfortable, supported, and like you make a difference within your workplace's work culture. Work culture includes the same kinds of things that define other cultures: attitudes and interactions, traditions and values, as well as leadership.

Have you ever asked yourself what really influences your decisions? Why do you prefer one workplace over another? For instance, why do you prefer being employed by a company versus working on your own? Why do you live where you live right now? Or even, why are you with the person you are in a relationship with? Or why are you not in a relationship right now? Some of us think it's all serendipity—that things happen, and we flow along with life. Other people think they set goals and then deliberately make those goals happen.

Think about it this way. The goal of a resume is to get an interview, and the goal of the interview is to get an offer. Whether you get an offer or not, focus on practicing interviewing. Most of us don't marry the first person we date. We practice to learn what kind of person fits. This is the same with interviewing. I'm not suggesting that we interview just for the sake of interviewing, but the more we practice asking our important questions and learn how to read the answers, the more likely we are to get what we ultimately want.

Keep in mind, however, that if the only questions you ask are self-serving, you may miss out on a great work opportunity. Every question you ask signals something to the potential employer, so choose carefully. I suggest putting yourself in the interviewer's shoes. What kinds of questions inspire confidence that a potential employee would be a good fit for the job you have open? What about this employee is making you trust them? Trust is the cornerstone of hiring. The reason you hear that "people hire people who are like them" is because they believe (correctly or incorrectly) that they can trust the person because they believe they understand them. The decisions this person will make will reflect well on them as the boss. If you want to be hired, you need to let the interviewer know that you can be trusted.

Asking questions to shed light on a company's culture is best when it's not stated or perceived as a demand. That can leave a negative impression. The first interview is not the time to be telling the interviewer all the things you want. This is the time to ask questions and listen carefully.

I recommend jotting down the exact words the hiring manager uses in response to your questions. In the pressure of the moment, you might mishear or misunderstand. Being able to refer to the exact wording can be helpful. After the interview, reread the words. You might be pleasantly or unpleasantly surprised about the impression you have about the company and the people with whom you interviewed.

Formulating Interview Questions

There are three steps to preparing to ask solid questions about culture. Different people want different things from an employment situation. Some people may want a place where they can have a social life with work colleagues. Some people are more interested in learning or skillbuilding. Here are the steps to help identify a company's culture:

1. Take your top three values that you identified in chapter 5 as the most important for you in finding meaningful work.
2. Research and objectively assess what you can find out about the organization's culture.
3. Translate your values into interview questions.

Step 1: Knowing Your Values

If you haven't yet worked through your personal values, I encourage you to go back and work on chapter 5. Without a clear understanding and prioritization of your values, assessing fit is harder. The best way to ensure that you find meaningful work is to understand the values that underpin your sense of self.

If working through that exercise isn't your thing, I suggest you review a list of values and pick your top three to five. While it's not as effective as doing a more thoughtful analysis, it will get you started on the process of evaluating organizations for compatible values.

Once you have identified your three to five top core values, you have an appropriate starting point.

Step 2: Assessing an Organization's Culture

The initial step in assessing a company's culture is to understand the elements of workplace culture. Paul Spiegelman, considered an expert on workplace culture, wrote an article for *Inc.* called "10 Elements of Great Company Culture"[23] that serves as a good start. Key components to focus on are community and core values.

Community

Let's consider the following as cornerstones of community:

- Camaraderie
- Celebrations
- Caring
- Connection

These concepts are good starting points from which to learn more about how much the organization values the connection between management and employees. It's easy for an employer to say that creating a community is important. It is another thing to build policies and actions that help create it.

You may have experienced honest community building at your church, with your hobbies, or during your volunteer work. People in these communities genuinely feel that their efforts have meaning and are valued. Connections between people are nurtured. If you have had this experience, you know what it feels like. You know when it's genuine and when it's fake. An organization may be learning and trying to build a community. It may understand its importance but may not yet have successfully attained its goal. Effort and intention mean a lot. This is in contrast to the company that says all the right things but doesn't really care.

Core Values

Company values are generally built on the story of the founders. The smaller the company, the more important the story is. If it's clear that a company has been founded with the goal of selling it off to make money, the culture may be less important than one where founders stay in control.

Consistency also matters.

- Are the core values the same today as they were at the start?
- Do leaders behave as if their voice, opinions, and decisions are the most important, or are they able to take input from employees?

The larger the organization, the more difficult it is to read intentions, as laws and regulations can interfere with good intentions. By researching, interviewing, and experimenting, you will improve your ability to know what works best for you.

Benefits Do Not (Necessarily) Equal Core Values

It can be easy to mistake certain benefits for core values. A free lunch isn't a core value. Using a free lunch to spend time with employees and learn about them, however, might indicate a core value of connection. If the reason your employer helps you with a gym membership is because it lowers their health care cost, that doesn't make it a core value. If the gym membership is part of a genuine effort to make sure employees are healthy and happy, however, then well-being may be important to the company.

Some core values are:

- Trust
- Commitment to customers
- Fun
- Continuous learning
- Diversity
- Sustainability

If you were going to start a company, which of these values would be the most important to you? All values cannot be equally important. It would be great if they could be, but that's not practical. We need to put some values higher than others so we can take action on the most important ones and judge an organization's effort in that area.

Understanding and prioritizing our own values and then understanding those of the employer can help us compare values in a more meaningful way.

And Now...a Story

JORDAN EVALUATES FIT

Jordan is especially interested in learning opportunities. In their current job, they thought there were going to be chances to use an educational reimbursement benefit that the company offered. When accepting the job, Jordan didn't ask any specific questions about this benefit but assumed they would be able to use it. It turned out this benefit was only available to certain employees under certain circumstances. Jordan wasn't eligible to use it.

Jordan wanted to learn about financials and thought that they would try to talk to their supervisor about it. During their discussion, Jordan's boss indicated that they were not "ready" to allow Jordan to take on this kind of assignment. Jordan doesn't want a repeat of this at any new gig they might consider taking.

Here are some draft questions that Jordan might have asked when interviewing for a new job (and then listened carefully to the answers, jotting down verbatim responses):

- ★ How are employees shown they are valued?
- ★ How are opportunities for learning identified and shared?
- ★ What is the company's turnover rate (how long do employees stay at this company)?
- ★ When employees stay, what kinds of career paths might they follow?
- ★ What kind of training or educational opportunities are offered? (If the choices are limited, then maybe this organization is more interested in what Jordan can do for it than growing together as employer/employee.)

In addition to those questions, here are some general questions about how the company thinks and acts toward employees that will help Jordan understand the core values of the company:

- ★ What kinds of flexibility are there in benefits? Do all employees get the same benefits?

★ Does the company have flexible scheduling?

★ Is there a dress code, even an unwritten one?

★ Are there any employee community-building activities (lunches, softball, etc.)?

★ How does company management address differences in work styles?[24] (Large organizations often provide training for employees in various learning or work styles to improve the way people communicate and work together. Myers-Briggs is one of the tools that is used for self and team style evaluations. If you work in a small company, this kind of training may not be available. It is in the best interest of any organization to help employees learn about working together.)

Step 3: Translating Values into Interview Questions

As an interviewee, you probably know the questions to ask about the job itself. If not, then I suggest you do some research. Ask friends, a mentor, or people in your industry what kinds of questions will help you quickly assess whether the work "fits" your skills and requirements.

"Understanding and prioritizing our own values and then understanding those of the employer can help us compare values in a more meaningful way."

More difficult is knowing what questions to ask to assess a company's cultural fit for your core values. Understanding your own values and knowing which questions to ask are two parts of the equation, but there are also three other important parts: knowing how and when to ask the questions, watching body language, and listening to the answers.

Your Questions

Depending on the length of the interview, you may want to limit the number of questions you ask. Don't be afraid to ask five questions, depending on the length of the answers. Ten questions might be too many for a short interview. Use your common sense. Ask if you can call later if more questions come up. Prioritize your most important questions to be sure they get addressed.

Here are some questions for consideration:

- What was the most recent big accomplishment or milestone (and how was it celebrated)? How are successes celebrated here?
- What's one thing you would change about the company if you could?
- How and when is performance feedback given?
- Do employees have a voice in any company decisions?
- It's one year from now... How would you measure success of the company? Success in the role I'm applying for? Or how do employees measure the success or impact of their work?
- Who would be my direct supervisor? [Never assume you know who it is.] Who would write my performance appraisal? [If they don't do performance appraisals, how will you get a raise—on somebody's whim, or is everyone in the company given the same amount at the same time?]
- Thinking of the last person who had this job, where did that person go after leaving this job? Or where do people in this role typically move on to?
- How often do projects get canceled?
- Where does the company see itself in five years?

My favorite question is, why is this a great place to work? I watch the person's body language; it quickly tells me whether they think it's a great place to work. Jot down the exact wording of their answer. When I ask this question of each person I interview with and review the exact wording each person uses, I get another view of the organization.[25]

How and When to Ask These Questions

Put yourself in the shoes of the interviewer. Imagine you have two candidates; one inspires confidence by asking well-thought-out questions about the job and the company, and the other spends most of their time talking about what they need and want. To which candidate would you make a job offer? This may be an extreme example, but you get the point. It is wise to consider when and how to ask questions related to culture.

Many hiring managers like to control the interview. After all, it's their job. If they feel like they are being "grilled," you may get the opposite result of what you want. However, if you don't ask questions concerning cultural fit, you may end up wasting valuable time jumping from job to job, aggravated by being confronted with the same issues again and again. It's all about balance.

Of course, there is no guarantee that you will be able to ferret out the truth about the intentions of a future employer. It can be complicated to know what questions to ask to get a true assessment of, for instance, how the team works together. When I ask an employer if their organization encourages teamwork, they will of course say yes. If I ask them how important teamwork is to the organization, they will say, "Very important." But if I ask them how they encourage teamwork or how they let employees know that teamwork is important, I might receive an answer as detailed as my personal values, or I might catch them without an answer or with an insincere answer if it's not a significant part of the work culture.

A Few More Tips...

- Practice being an active listener. Repeat back the interviewer's key points to show you are listening and understanding. This practice also shows that you can process information correctly. It is a good skill to demonstrate when you want to be trusted and is an excellent skill in general.
- Offer a firm handshake. A "dead fish" handshake does not inspire confidence. A firm handshake communicates self-assurance.
- Look people in the eye. This may take practice. You don't want to stare people down, but you also don't want to look at the floor. Eye contact shows confidence, and confidence is often equated with competence.

And Now...Another Story

JESS LEARNS TO ASK AND CLARIFY

Flexible scheduling is an important factor for Jess, who has a job interview tomorrow. They are excited about the opportunity but have been burned before by jobs that sound good but turn out to be entry-level and boring. Jess wants to make sure not only that the job is interesting but that they will have time to practice guitar and perform at gigs.

Jess wants to work 7:00 a.m. to 4:00 p.m. but had two unfruitful experiences asking for these hours in interviews at two different companies:

- ★ Interview 1—The hiring manager said no. There would be no discussion about it.
- ★ Interview 2—Human Resources indicated that a flexible work schedule was part of the benefits package. What Jess didn't hear or write down but remembered afterward was the unfortunate key: "at the supervisor's discretion."

Jess took the second job, expecting to be able to negotiate hours on their first day. When they started working, their new boss said that this benefit didn't apply to their work area. Jess protested but was met with "Sorry, there's nothing we can do."

Frustrated by these experiences, Jess knew they needed a new approach, to ask more straightforward questions such as:

- ★ What percent of employees work a flexible schedule?
- ★ Does the company perceive that flexible scheduling contributes to productivity?
- ★ Does my work group have hours where everyone is expected to be at work?

If the interviewer isn't sure, ask them to check. In your acceptance letter, state that you heard from the exact person you spoke with that this group had flexible scheduling and that you were looking forward to a schedule that would work for the group and yourself. By stating this in the acceptance letter, you have reinforced what you have been told and what is important to you.

It's very important to watch the interviewer's body language. When you ask these questions, do they look you in the eye or look at the floor? Do their shoulders slump slightly? Are they truly enthusiastic, or are they faking it?

A Word about Responsibly Earning a Living

If money is the main motivator for why you work, you may struggle to find that less traveled road to meaningful work. All of us need money, but if your number one value and work goal are to make a lot of money, then you may find some of this unnecessary.

I'm all for being fairly compensated for my effort and talent. I like money and the choices I have as a result of managing it well. How we spend our money each day is a choice. When we're young, we may spend money we don't have or continue to ask for money from parents without much thought. I understand. But this is what I came to learn: discipline is freedom. This may sound contradictory—if I'm free, why do I need discipline? The truth is that unless we are born wealthy, and even if we are, money will always be a struggle of some kind. The sooner we come to grips with our spending, saving, and managing debt, the sooner we are free from the weight of having "money problems."

We are each free to handle our money any way we choose. Responsibly earning a living means that we live on what we make. We don't require someone else to provide for our basic living expenses. There may be all kinds of reasons why this is difficult (illness, disability, etc.). Be honest with yourself about your actions with regards to money. Are you being responsible to yourself? Only you know the answer. In the You Work It section, I offer the idea of a money audit. See if that interests you.

Resources to Help You Assess Company Culture

- ☞ Check out Glassdoor (glassdoor.com). Among resources for learning about potential employers, Glassdoor is particularly useful, if used cautiously. It allows employees to post information about pay, advancement, and atmosphere of their employer. As with all review or rating sites, take this information with a grain of salt. In other words, we don't know the motives for an employee writing a review. Take the information and add it to other research you've done about the organization.
- ☞ Speak candidly with a current or recent employee. Even if the person doesn't say anything specific, you likely can tell whether their experience is or was positive or negative.
  Remember that even if this person says terrible things about an employer, that doesn't mean that company might not work for you. Unless you can mutually identify with the goals and values of the person evaluating the employer, you need to keep an open mind. Key values like safety, honesty, ethics, etc., are universally important, but others appeal to different people in varying importance. Also remember that the employee with whom you are talking worked for a person at that company. Their supervisor's behavior may not reflect on the company as a whole. Trust yourself to know the difference between someone who's trying to shuffle blame to someone else and someone who has a legitimate concern. Take notes when talking to people about a particular

employer. Write down phrases verbatim, so when you think back, you can be sure you're remembering their words correctly and not interpreting their words through your brain's filter.

💎 Comparably (comparably.com) and CareerBuilder (careerbuilder.com) were built primarily to help job hunters understand an organization's pay scale. If you are serious about a company or a job, check out as many of these resources as you can. Don't forget to look at the financials for a potential employer. Are they private or public? Even if you only have access to revenues and net income, you'll have an idea of the solvency of a future employer.

MEANINGFUL CASE WORK STUDY

Where did you grow up?

A rural area in northern California.

What did your parents do for a living?

Dad was a park ranger back when rangers were naturalists. He was very enthusiastic about his work. My dad retired after thirty years and went back to school to get a master's in museum studies and became the curator of a little museum near where we lived.

My mom had a wide variety of jobs from server to teaching assistant to health food store clerk. She was always passionate about what she did, and I remember her saying that it doesn't matter what job you're doing—you can always find something that you love in what you do. Today, my mom works with at-risk teens at a health and rehabilitation center. Most of the kids have been on the streets. It's pretty intense work. Where we lived strongly influenced the kind of work both my parents did. There weren't many choices, but they both loved what they did.

Tell us about your educational background.

I went to college and graduated in four years (many people take longer), but I incurred a lot of debt. I originally thought I wanted to be a veterinarian, but then I didn't like the classes, so I switched to sociology with an environmental focus. I was passionate about the subject and graduated with that degree, but I had no idea what I was going to do. I was concerned about paying back my loans but decided I would figure it out.

H's journey to finding meaningful work:

Before finding the job I have today, I worked at several jobs where I didn't feel like a human. I felt like I wasn't valued for the things I could bring to the table and my ideas and thoughts didn't matter. I was there to do a job, and that was it. I worked as a server and a store clerk. When I worked these jobs, I felt crappy and was treated poorly. I was another number who wasn't moving fast enough.

However, while at one of those jobs, I became friends with someone who taught me how to manage money. As soon as I got a paycheck, she told me to put as much as I could into a savings account; it didn't matter if it was just three dollars—just put it in there. As my job and pay increased, I increased the amount of money I put away. I ended up saving almost $1,000 in one month because I found myself with extra cash. I would have liked to spend it on something, but I knew if I could continue saving, I would get out from under my loans. My mind is blown—I'm now twenty-eight, and my loans are paid!

My friend taught me about handling my money, but interestingly, she hates her job. She's worked there for a million years. She's not fond of the people, and she finds the work boring. She gets benefits and time off but is so unhappy. At first, that's what I thought jobs should be like—I should show up, hate my job, and as long as I was getting paid, stay there.

In my next job, I worked at a veterinary company. This job was really important to me; I saw that it wasn't necessary to hate the work I'm doing and that what mattered was that I cared about my coworkers and they cared about me. I learned that I am the kind of person who needs to enjoy my job.

Now, I work at food co-op. We sell wonderful things, mostly local, organic food. I started in a fairly low-level position; then I became an assistant manager, then front-end manager. I was moving up and making good money, but I could see it wasn't a good long-term fit for me. I put a lot of money into savings, which was great, but the job was taking its toll on me. What I had observed was that what the store needed most was someone who could answer customer questions, someone with a broad understanding of the store and our products—basically a "store support" position. I put in a proposal to my boss to create a new position. I wrote up the description and worked to get the support of key people for the utility of this function. I ended up having to apply for the job and got it!

I love my job. I have been trained in every department in the store. I feel like I'm part of a caring community and serving something greater than myself. That's what's really important to me. I'm not just working to find a box of something for someone but to engage with people who believe in good food and want to support a good place to shop. The community feels very caring. I know and love the people who shop here. I can tell you about the generations of a family who all shop here; John and Carol are the grandparents, and then I know their daughter Susan and her husband and daughter. I know that Janet is finishing her graduate program, and Eric is meeting his family back East for a reunion. I can tell you who got married because they came in and asked me about the pies for their wedding. I love feeling a part of something; it's really beautiful to me. The people I work with see me and value me as a human, and I can bring all my skills to work every day. They know that I am good at listening and relating to people. They encourage me to be myself and bring my whole self to serve our community.

Thinking back on my job transitions, as I was stepping down from my job [as front-end manager], even though I knew I was going into a new, better job [that I'd created myself], I felt like I was failing, and that was scary. I was leaving a job where I had authority, and now, I wouldn't have that. I was stepping down to the bottom of the barrel. I was making less money, and it felt like a loss of status. I was scared that the change was going to be too difficult to deal with. However, my sanity required that I do something different. Interestingly, I found more joy and more connection to customers and coworkers in this new position, and that decision was one of the best moves I've ever made.

Every day, I look for the purpose in what I do, even if it's repetitive. I'm there for my community, and for me, this is the key to meaningful work. I care more about the people and the feeling of being useful than I do the societal values of money and status.

There's no "career track" in this position. There are no other stores for me to go to implement this same change. But it still feels like the right thing for me because, now, I love going to work every day. I feel valued and cared about as a human being.

Imagine an ideal work environment.

1. Write down the things that are important to you in a workplace. To get ideas, ask friends what kinds of work environments they like. Keep a running list, adding to it as appropriate (for example, the things you want and need as a single person will be different from what you need when you have your first child).

2. What are some of your values that might influence your fit at work (religion, money, honesty, etc.)?

3. Once you have those two lists, formulate questions you might ask in an interview or when you are learning about a potential employer that would help determine whether there's fit.

   For instance, let's say your values are as follows:

   - Effectiveness
   - Independence
   - Respect
   - Teamwork
   - Curiosity

   Questions you might ask could be:

   - How often are goals set and measured for individual performers (versus team or project)?
   - How are employee disagreements resolved?
   - What learning initiatives are popular right now?

   Remember, when you ask these questions, be sure to not only listen for an answer but watch for body language to gauge if the interviewer is prepared for the question and is genuine in their answer.

4. Conduct a money audit on yourself. If you are living above your means, it might be helpful to do a money audit to

identify you spending habits. There are several of these online. If you would like to feel better about your money situation, use tools that help you:

    a. Assess how you spend your money today.

    b. Find a way to make it easy to know where your money goes (regularly review your finances).

    c. Identify unproductive (to your financial goals) spending patterns (takeout, retail therapy, etc.).

    d. Make a plan to understand your money habits.

    e. Get help from a trusted resource.

CHAPTER 13

YOU'RE IN!
HOW TO THRIVE
IN YOUR NEW POSITION

ongratulations! You assessed, interviewed, and got the offer. Are you feeling excited? Nervous? Looking forward to learning? Meeting new people? To varying degrees, we all feel these emotions when we start a new job. What separates someone who is successful in their new job from someone who struggles? One factor may be how they navigate their first three to four months. Our early behavior with our boss, our colleagues, and others directly impacts how these people perceive us and treat us in the coming days, months, and years.

I estimate I've had about thirty-five paying jobs. Eliminating gigs before and during college leaves me with having started about twenty new jobs. I learned a few things about how to handle myself in these early days of a new environment. I hope my experience will help make your new job experience less nerve-racking.

Before Accepting the Offer

We seldom have more negotiating power than after we receive an offer and before we accept the job. Once we know the organization has chosen us, we have the chance to ask for what we want. If our list of "demands" is too long, the offer might evaporate. But if we accept a job without any negotiation, we lose the best chance we have of getting what we want and need to make this job a great fit. A solid negotiation also shows your employer that you are confident enough to know what you want and to ask for it.

What you negotiate is up to you. Keep your goals in mind when you think about your requests. But do negotiate something.

When people complain to me that they didn't get the raise they believe they deserved, I ask them what they negotiated about raises prior to accepting the job. They typically say, "I didn't." I'm not someone who likes to negotiate or thinks it's fun. I had to learn how to do it and then make myself do it. After all, since I know my contribution will be valuable, it's up to me to get the best deal I can regarding my money, time, and energy.

For example, if you want schedule flexibility and you ask for it, think about what you'll do if they say no. I have been prepared to turn the offer down if I didn't get the flexibility I required. If your potential employer says no to all your reasonable proposals, you may not be valued in a way that you would like.

Honestly, it's tricky. If you ask for too many things, the employer may decide you're too much trouble and rescind the offer. This is why it is so important to be clear about what is important to you and then determine what you can get. My approach was that I am not entitled to a flexible schedule—I'm asking for it. I want to make it a win-win. Rest assured, however, that employers expect new hires to negotiate. Research information on negotiating to help give you ideas, but these won't help you know what to ask for. That's up to you.

Your First Days (and Months) on the Job

When I would start a new job, I would be eager to impress. I would dive in, ask a lot of questions, offer ideas and suggestions, and tell everyone how we did it at my old job.

I hope you're smarter than I was.

It takes time to get to know your new colleagues, company politics, and priorities. The first few weeks are a time to ask questions and to listen. Yes, you want to be respected, but keep in mind that they hired you—so in many cases, you already are. Yes, you have to earn continued respect, but you are better able to do this if you take stock of the people you work for and with, investigate ways to be part of the team, and listen for the heartbeat of the new place. A heartbeat might be different from one place to another. At some places it's how much money is being made. At others, it's all about an individual's ability to get ahead. In other places, there's a commitment to the mission that feeds the energy of the team.

I learned to give myself three months to settle in. That doesn't mean that you should wait to make a contribution—absolutely not. But tell yourself to relax and check things out. You can be friendly but not too friendly. After all, this is work. As much as you might bond with your coworkers, the job is your livelihood. It takes time to understand the company's values, learn what makes the organization tick, and determine who has the power (hint: it's not always the person you think or with the fancy title). This requires subtle detective work.

Understand Expectations

The best way to understand the expectations of you and your role is to ask. Get clear about the needs of your direct supervisor so that you can meet or exceed them whenever you can. Put these expectations in writing and discuss them with your boss. Ask if you have understood what's expected. I learned to have a regular check-in with my boss. These check-ins were suggested and managed by me; they can be casual, brief conversations that will give you a way of making sure you won't be surprised by your boss's assessment of your work.

Some organizations have formal processes for discussing performance; others have none. Either way, it is important to know how you are doing and where you stand. I encourage you to think about connecting with your direct supervisor in this casual but important way.

Unfortunately, some bosses are inaccessible. There's no getting around this. If you find yourself in this position, it may be OK. If you can find benefit from working on your own without much support, then go for it. The boss/subordinate relationship can be awkward, even when the people are the "same" (people tend to hire people that are like them). Early on in our careers, it's useful to have bosses and mentors who recognize our authentic selves, but toxic bosses are hard to avoid. If we find ourselves with one of these, it's important to get extra outside support so we don't lose faith in ourselves. At the end of the day, what's important is that we know ourselves for who we are. Valuable, precious, and unique.

Tips for When You Start Working

1. Be clear about what results you are being asked to deliver. Be realistic yet confident about your contribution.
2. Schedule check-ins (and make sure they happen) with your boss to make sure that things are going well. Don't count on the fact that you haven't heard any complaints.
3. Make a point of saying to your boss at regular intervals, "How am I doing?" Listen openly to the feedback. Do not become defensive; that's not in your best interest. Actively listen to what is being said and be sure you understand the concerns. Promise to respond in a day or two, in writing, with recommendations to improve the situation.

4. Do the same thing with employees and coworkers with whom you work closely. Head off problems by being proactive and responsive.

Corporate Politics (The Game)

An unfortunate but real part of work is politics. Understand the "game" of politics in the workplace—how it is played and your role in it—and you have a fighting chance of surviving it. Of course, you can choose to ignore the game, considering it stupid, useless, or beneath you. I understand those feelings. I would hope that, at least, you would understand how politics came to be such an important part of the business world. Would you play checkers without knowing the rules? It wouldn't be much fun if you did. If you play or watch sports, you know how important it is to understand the game and its objectives.

If you find yourself in a place where games are minimal, congratulations. For most of us, there will be various levels of gamesmanship. I'm not judging whether politics is a good or bad thing. While some of it is petty, perhaps some of it is necessary. Knowledge is power in this case.

While in my mid-thirties, I was fortunate to have a mentor who helped me with my career. His wife had been mentored into one of the highest-level positions at the Fortune 25 corporation where I worked. I learned a great deal from him (thank you, Bob!). He was a vice president of the division I worked in. He gave me a book to read called *Games Mother Never Taught You*, by Betty Harragan. This book changed how I viewed the world of work forever. Without Bob and the opportunities he helped me find, I would not be the businessperson I am today.

Some of the content of the book (published in 1970) is outdated, but a lot of what it describes is still valid. A key takeaway for me was the evolution of the modern workplace and the rules of the game are based on military structure. Hierarchies, chain of command, operational versus staff positions, etc., are all concepts and structures borrowed directly from the armed services. Professional sports also adopted this infrastructure in creating the "rules" of the game. If you understand something about the military, you will have a better insight into how business works.

In addition, the way males and females were raised in the past (it's improved...) and trained also affected how organizations view employees. The masculine personality will take a job as a "challenge," while the feminine counterpart will speculate about whether she has the right credentials or training to take on that same assignment. My experience is that feminine-personality job seekers who are vastly more qualified than others, hesitate to pursue interesting, valuable work because they are afraid of failing. If you understand this element of the game and how the rules have affected you, you have a better chance of playing to your advantage. Without understanding the rules of the politics at your workplace, you might be disadvantaged when your team is playing a different game than you are.

If you understand sports, use that knowledge to understand your new environment. Ask for an organization chart. If there isn't one, make your own. The benefit of spending time understanding the "players" in the game is that if and when you decide to engage (for example, ask for a raise, an opportunity, or a promotion), you have a head start. Finding meaningful work means taking responsibility for our own future. We can engage in learning about the people, or we can ignore them. The problem with ignoring "the game" is that we may become a victim of the game, for example, become stuck in a dead-end job, working for an uncaring boss, for lousy pay. Those things might happen if we *do* find out about the people, but at least we did what we could and learned in the process.

Power in the Workplace

Millennials and Gen Zers have a keen sense of authenticity. You all are much better at spotting a phony than I was. Your generational radar is well-tuned, but not all baby boomers appreciate that you notice and even call them on their affected or self-serving behavior. It's important for you to learn about your new workplace and be careful with whom and how you share that information. You're better off talking with someone with solid business experience outside your company versus a coworker.

As you are gathering information about the company leadership, you will also learn about other influential people in the organization. It's not always about job titles. There are a number of sources of power in a workplace. As you get to know people, note who influences the people and organization beyond their apparent title, position, or function.

As you attend meetings, be sure to identify all the people in the room. This is a good way to begin to learn about people. Listen to individuals. Watch body language. You will begin to understand who is charge—not who is running the meeting but who people defer to. When the power person talks, people take notes.

Here are different sources of power in a workplace:

- **Positional power or one-way vertical power (flows down)**—In this organizational hierarchy, the CEO has more positional power than the financial officer or other members of the management team. Your manager has positional power over you. This type of power used to be the most significant source of power in organizations. Not anymore. Why? Because certain types of expertise, for example, technical, can push a company one way or another based on products, services, customers, or funding.

  Exercising positional power ("because I told you to do it") to get those employees "beneath" them to do what they want, is a weak position. Managing by fear or intimidation is the laziest and least effective tool in a manager's tool kit.

- **Influence power (flows side to side or upward)**—This type of power emanates from people who are clear about the path forward and/or who have credentials that make their opinions matter. They influence people to achieve based on sharing a vision and getting people to buy in. Workers follow this individual because they respect them. A great leader helps workers feel that their voice matters. In a growing firm, it's useful for any person, regardless of position, to make suggestions and influence strategy. This type of power emerges from the strength of the person's personality, charisma, or credentials. If the CEO happens to be charismatic or, for instance, technically competent, it can be a good thing. I say it "can be" because charismatic or skilled subject-matter people can be lousy leaders too.

- **Connection power**—This person may be a friend or relative of the people in power. They may be the kind of person who can cultivate relationships with ease and knows how to work those connections to their advantage. This is a skill. Some people work at being personable and building contacts; for others, it happens unconsciously. These people are respected because they have relationships that support their standing.

There is no need to judge these different sources of power; what's important is to observe them so that you know who is moving the organization forward. This information is useful when thinking about who and how you are influenced at work. People who use positional power to manage teams are weak. In my experience, these people, who often identify as male, have limited communication and leadership tool kits. They influence by intimidation.

There aren't many ways to get around positional power if your boss uses this as a primary management strategy. For non-boss individuals who use their positions like hammers, here are a few tools for influencing them:

- ☙ **Build a wide network of people** who know and respect you and who you know and respect. This is the most effective way to gain influence and protect yourself from higher-ups with an agenda. Earning the esteem of a wide range of people, in all walks of life, is an interesting and pleasant way to live life, and you may be amazed at how these individuals might help you when you least expect it.

- ☙ **Stand a little closer.** This isn't a strategy to be used by everyone, but when I did choose to use it, I was delighted with the outcome. Every country and culture has norms regarding personal space, how close to stand to another person. In a subordinate relationship, eye contact and physical proximity have norms that exist even if we aren't consciously aware of them.

   It can be unnerving for a positional power player to have their space invaded. They believe (or are hoping) they are intimidating others into doing what they want. When I would invade their space, ever so slightly, I sent a subtle signal that I wasn't afraid.

   In my case, I would take half a step into the space between myself and the intimidator, usually to their side. If you try this, you may notice that the other person takes a half step back, or they may hold their ground. Either way, you will sense their discomfort. Alternatively, they may take another half step toward you.

   This is a risky strategy not to be used by or on everyone. Never use this on people weaker than you or people who work for you. Never use it lightly.

   It's subtle, but it can backfire; the person might get very upset, and if they feel defensive, it may work against you. If you are a tall person, this strategy can also be problematic. You already have a height advantage over most people, so trying to intimidate people by invading their space will likely have the opposite effect of what you're going for. Also, be careful that this move is not perceived as you making a romantic or sexual advance on the other person. Moving a bit closer to someone *could* be interpreted as something other than what you intended. Tread carefully.

- ☙ **Have a backup plan.** This may be the hardest part of today's living. Many millennials and Gen Zers have debt. Maybe you are thinking:

- ⊕ I owe too much money.
- ⊕ I can't find another job in my field.
- ⊕ I can't find another job that is convenient to get to.

You may have other concerns. These are formidable obstacles. I get it. It's not easy to change the way we think, plan, and act. I encourage you to be proactive when it comes to your work. I hope you won't settle for doing work that doesn't feed you. I hope you've found some tools and ideas in this book that will help you find the work that gives your life not just money but also satisfaction in how you spend your time and energy. Go back to part 1 of this book if you need new ideas.

Pick Your Battles

For better or worse, when I think I'm right, I am willing to push the point to prove it. Am I competitive? I don't think of myself that way, but maybe I am. It's just that it seems logical to get the answer right. However, reality is that "right" is in the eye of the one who holds the power. Not 100 percent of the time, but a lot of the time. I had to learn that, in the workplace, it isn't about being right—it is about being effective. If I wanted to be effective in my job and get the flexibility and credibility I desired, I had to learn to carefully select the topic and time to suggest that I had a better answer.

Initially, it seemed that I only had two choices: either I was right, and I was saying so directly to the other person, or I was right and just kept quiet. This was faulty logic. I had several choices; I had to learn to know them and use them to my advantage.

Among the choices are:

- ⊕ **"I'm wrong."** I think I'm right, but the reality is, I don't have all the facts the way someone, such as a superior, does. I learned to stop being so sure. It takes confidence to be wrong graciously. It's easier to be gracious when we haven't been cocky.
- ⊕ **"Let's agree to disagree."** This works sometimes, but I had to learn to be careful. It works in my personal life better than professionally. Since there is a power dynamic at work, I have to be clear about who I am challenging. And yes, many people will interpret "Let's agree to disagree" as a challenge to their power.

- ☙ **"How important is it?"** Everything isn't equally important. What's important is my peace of mind and my energy not being wasted. I decided it was more important to be happy than right. This helped me decide when to take on a battle and when to let it go. It's not weakness to let something go when I know that I have a good reason for doing so.

- ☙ **Stand my ground.** When I think that something is truly wrong (for example, discrimination, unethical behavior, harassment), I know it's time to stop and think about an approach. If I challenge this type of behavior without a plan, I may find myself in a sticky, no-win situation. This is why studying managers and other influential employees from day one at a job can be helpful. If you find out that unacceptable behavior is fully acceptable at your new workplace, then acknowledge that to yourself. Some battles are winnable...for some, the odds are long. Understand, with an open heart and mind, what you are up against. Yes, there are laws that protect unacceptable behavior from occurring. That doesn't mean that it doesn't go on. Follow your head and your heart.

- ☙ **Renew my focus on what I can control.** The more I pay attention to my own lane—mind my own business, focus on my productivity—the better. There are things that need to change in any environment. But am I the one that needs to change them? Are there ways to work to change the important things and let the rest go?

- ☙ **Offer a solution.** My rule has always been, don't go to the boss with a problem that I don't have a least one solution for. It may not have been the answer, but it showed that I had thought about solving the dilemma, and I was not just griping about it. Equally important is offering a few choices. People like choices. Whether they pick one of those offered isn't important. The decision maker feels empowered that they have alternatives. I don't offer any choice that I don't think I can live with. If the organization chooses a path forward that is problematic for me, that's the price I pay for trying to change things. Alternatively, not changing things may be worse. To just live with inefficiency, waste, lack of effort, or whatever the issue is hard.

- ☙ **Am I willing to do more than complain?** More than once, when I picked a battle, the solution became something for me to do on top of my other work. This isn't what I wanted. I wanted someone else to fix it. Part of raising the issue is being aware that it might become part of your work. This is why it needs to be important to you before you bring it up.

❧ **Realize that not all business decisions are rational.** This may sound strange, but I promise, some business decisions are made based on people having:

- ❧ A bad day
- ❧ Trouble at home
- ❧ Health problems
- ❧ The strong need or desire for power or money

The more you are aware of this, the less offended I hope you'll be when that lack of logic affects something important to you.

MEANINGFUL CASE WORK STUDY

Where did you grow up?

Upstate New York

What did your parents do for a living?

My mother's a nurse. She paid for her own education. Women back then had three choices if they wanted to work: health care (they could be nurses, not doctors), secretaries, or teachers. She gravitated toward health care because she loves people.

My father didn't go to college. He's entrepreneurial and has been self-employed most of his working life. He kept reinventing himself: snowplowing, painting, power washing—he's done it all.

Tell us about your educational background?

My guidance counselor told me I had to go to college and that whatever I studied was what I'd be doing the rest of my life. That was the most terrifying thing anybody could have ever said to me. Do one thing for the rest of my life? I was bad at test taking and ended up getting a terrible 970 on my SATs; doors were closing all around me as people told me I'd never make it in college.

I became very determined to show everybody I was better than what they were saying about me. My confidence was low, but in my heart, I knew I could do it. I decided to try community college. I looked at the course catalog and saw visual communications. I'd never heard of that. It was described as filmmaking (I'd been fooling around with my dad's camcorder since I was in high school), radio, and television production. Wow. That all sounds cool, I thought. I decided to talk to the people in the department. The woman I met that day would help change my life forever. She said, "Here are your courses. I'll see you when school starts."

I was in her video-and-television production classes; it was the best thing that ever could have happened to me. I didn't have to explain myself to other people. I could just blurt out an idea, and someone would pick up on it, and then we would create it. I graduated and was the first person ever from my community college to get into NYU Tisch School of the Arts.

V's journey to finding meaningful work:

When I was in the second grade, I saw a heart-shaped ring with my birthstone and really wanted it—but it was ninety-nine dollars. My father said I had to earn the money myself. So, I started mowing lawns and entertaining people. Coin by coin, I made ninety-nine dollars. I got the ring but then lost it doing cartwheels. However, I learned the value of working and one of its rewards—money. Throughout high school, I had probably three to four jobs at any given time; I was always working. During my senior year, I got a paid internship at a local corporation. I left school midmorning to go to work. It was terrible because here I was, this little free spirit, and everything was rigid. Women were treated differently (worse) than men. I needed the money, but I didn't last there long. My mother told me what you do professionally takes a lot of your life, and you should love what you do, or at least love something about what you do.

I finished undergrad and got a job with Viacom, working on unplugged music videos and the show *Law & Order*. It was my dream job. Then I fell in love, married a special forces soldier, and needed to leave New York City to return to my hometown. There, I got a job in the news department writing stories for the five o'clock news. However, my values didn't align with the job. I don't believe we have to report on destruction and fires and deaths. I didn't want to contribute content to the world that was so negative all the time; I wanted news to have a higher value.

I left that job and started another one as a secretary in the hospital, which felt like it had a higher purpose. In reality, I fielded calls from drug addicts who didn't want to talk to me; they wanted to talk to the doctor. It felt very much like a fall from grace; I was only in my early twenties, had already worked for MTV, doing interviews with people like Beyoncé, and now I was on the phone with drug addicts screaming at me. The silver lining was that I gained perspective about my ego.

Down the road, before I ended up getting divorced, I had the realization that I wanted to make more money than my husband. That became my new career goal. Finding work wasn't about getting another role in production; it wasn't about what I loved anymore.

It was about vindication on my finances. So, I became a financial advisor and got fully licensed. Before that, I didn't even know what a rate of return was. I got into an industry that was so foreign to me; I didn't have an economics background, and I didn't even like, nor was I good at math.

I had never done sales before either, and now I was a salesperson. But a very good friend of mine gave me some good advice: "Every opportunity is an opportunity to wear a new suit; it doesn't mean you have to keep the suit on forever—it just means you're going to try it on."

It was a very hard career for me; I made $17,000 my first year and $18,000 my next year. I exhausted most of the savings that I had, trying to build a business. Then I had a conversation with my aunt, who gave me a good recommendation to take my sales experience and my television experience and sell advertising for the local TV station. I made $35,000 that first year. When you're in the sales world, specifically for ad sales, they give you an account base to call when you first start. My account base was worth $20,000, so that would have been my income if I didn't bring in new business.

But as ambitious as I was, I could see that there was a plateau. I've always been very good at reading organizations and seeing the opportunity (or lack thereof). Because it was a small organization with very old sales staff with low turnover, I knew that I'd have to bring in major new business in a very saturated market.

The writing was on the wall. That was a moment where I had to decide what was next. My licenses were going to expire in the finance world when a friend of mine said there was a position open for a sales assistant with Morgan Stanley, starting at $55,000. I figured that was better than what I was making, although I really didn't want to sit behind a desk. I did like that it was a very large organization, and it also was an opportunity to get back to New York.

I've been with the firm for nearly five years now. I don't think I've ever been with a company, other than MTV, this long. I started as a sales assistant at twenty-six years old in October 2014. I talked to every person who came into the firm from New York City, networking internally, and eventually meeting my manager, who hired me as a producer. I then met somebody in the media department, who told me that they do a lot of video production, which I didn't even know existed in the firm. So, I got hired as a producer in New York—which had been my dream all along!

What are some lessons you've learned along the way?

Lesson 1 : Whatever job you're in, look for opportunities to set your soul on fire. For example, I love nature, and I love trees, so the amount of paper we used in the firm was really upsetting to me; I couldn't handle it. I was one of the younger sales support staff, so I wasn't all about "business as usual." One day, I got an email about e-sign, which is a program that allows clients to sign documents without using paper. I thought, oh my god, we could save so many trees! I became really passionate about it; I got up in meetings and talked to everybody about the opportunity and how they could come to my desk and I'd show them how to use it. For me, it's meaningful to work in a job where I can affect change, to the benefit of not only our clients but the world.

Storytelling also sets my soul on fire. Production makes for a very hard life. Most people think they can do my job without understanding how videos get made. They don't understand the components that make a really great story—the characters, narrative, music, etc., that inspire the audience. I come from a family of storytellers, so it comes naturally to me; I know how to get people engaged. Production is meaningful work to me because I feel it uses my skill set. Meaningful work, to me, not only sets your soul on fire but also empowers you to help other people get done what they need to get done. Take what you're really good at and be of service to others.

Lesson 2: When I went back to New York, I wanted to go back to producing content. I had tried selling and administrative work; it was time to go for what I loved. I'm working at an investment bank, making corporate videos. It's not riveting stuff, but it allows me the opportunity to be around people I feel are my professional soul sidekicks; I get to be on set and make an idea come to life, to pull pieces together and create something new. There's something magical about it that I've never been able to shake. I've lost lovers and friends because this is what sets my soul on fire, more than anything else. Every choice I made (even deciding I wanted to make more money than my husband) led me somewhere I wanted to be. Personal sacrifices can help pave the way to meaningful work.

Lesson 3: It's been tough being a woman in business. I've always been in very male-dominated industries; I started in media, which is 1,000 percent male-dominated. I had a female boss who would always pick on me: "Take your fingers out of your mouth." "Why are you biting your nails?" "Stop touching your hair like that." She kept nitpicking. Finally, one day I said to her, "What is your problem? Why do you constantly harp on me when I'm working?" She said, "Because I know you're going to be successful. I know you're going to get to the next level in your career, and I want you to understand that this is a male-dominated industry, and if you show any sign of weakness, you will get eaten alive." Point taken.

Even in my corporate environment today, Wall Street, I see her point. But there are positive things about this job too. I make a good wage for the work I do. I am learning a lot about business. The work does align with my values to some degree. I do have the feeling, however, when it comes to promoting women and people of color and being open, there's still a long way to go. I can't change the world, but I can make a contribution to making it better.

Another thing I've learned is that you have to take your career into your own hands. No one is guaranteed to help you. You have to say what it is you want, and then you have to act on it, day in and day out, no matter who or what gets in your way. There is no other way. You can't sit there and gossip or bitch and wait for things to get better.

You have to mitigate all sorts of roadblocks on your way to meaningful work. It's like when a bird comes by and shits on you; you just have to clean yourself off and keep going until you get to where you want to go. And then once you get there, keep in mind that you may discover what you thought was meaningful work for you, actually isn't. And that's OK. I've changed paths so many times because I'm a seeker. Which leads me to my next lesson...

Lesson 4: Nothing that you do in life is a mistake... There are just moments along your journey where you make choices that are right for you in that moment. And those choices are never lost. They come back to help you down the road when you least expect it. You'll say, "Geez, why did I just do that?" or "Why did I keep that job for four years?" Then, twelve years later, something will come up, and you'll have the skill set you'll need that you gained from that choice you made before. Everything comes full circle. You're not going to make a mistake, because there is no such thing.

Set yourself up for success.

Regardless of the culture/environment of your workplace, you are responsible for your own professional development. Here are some ways to get off to a great start in your new position:

1. **Write down your goals for the quarter, half year, and full year.** In some jobs, this will be easy; in others, it will be much harder. It's scary to write something down on paper because then you'll feel like you have to do it and will be held responsible if you don't. But the good news is that when you take responsibility for your goals, you are clear about your targets: your assignments, your output, and your professional growth. You have an idea about where you're going, and you have shared that with your boss. This takes extra effort, but it is totally worth it. Break your goals into three sections.
    a) Goals related to my current position
    b) Professional development goals
    c) Personal goals
   You don't have to share your progress or goals regarding all three sections at every meeting, but it's good to share them with your boss in order to demonstrate your competence, your acceptance of the responsibility for your career, and that you communicate your expectations.
2. **Set up a regular check-in meeting with your boss** and ask the question, "How am I doing?" Ask about expectations and indicate that every month or so you are going to ask for this informal feedback. The higher you rise in responsibilities, the more important this question will become. It takes the onus off your boss to find a good time to give you feedback. And, since you are asking the question, you will be mentally prepared if the feedback happens to be negative. After all, you asked for feedback. It's your responsibility to accept what your boss is saying and then figure out what to do next.

3. **Contribute outside the company.** This can manifest in many different ways. Here are a couple of examples of what I did in my career:
    a. **Published articles in relevant journals**—I would have an idea for an article and then pitch it to magazines related to my business. Some got accepted, and I was happy to write them.
    b. **Gave presentations**—I loved being a teacher and found I had a knack for speaking in front of people. The first time I spoke in front of hundreds of people, I was terrified. Frankly, I still get nervous talking in front of groups. But I knew that I was learning, I was making my company look good, and I had this to put on my list of accomplishments.

I hope you will find your way of contributing. It can make it easy on your boss to recommend you for that raise or opportunity.

CHAPTER 14

ENVISIONING FUTURE WORK

The definition of work was to make some original contribution to the world, and in the process not to starve. To be happy, I think you have to be doing something you not only enjoy but admire.
—**Paul Graham**, "How to Do What You Love"

This book is designed to help you know yourself and your choices—to broaden your perspective and help you believe in the power of your uniqueness. As you may recall from the introduction, this book is built around this equation:

My values (who I am at this point in my life)

+

My skills (current and those I hope to gain)

+

My available resources (people/tools)

+

My actions (experimenting, questioning, taking risks)

=

A path to meaningful work

I hope you can see that if you have worked through the exercises, you have a broad and useful foundation for finding work that feeds you, body and soul.

If you already had a vision for your future life before reading this book, I hope that it has provided some guidance and alternatives toward a more powerful and flexible vision of your future, meaningful work.

If you've done the earlier work in this book, you will find it easier to change the way you think about finding work. If you haven't, test the tools in this chapter for if and how they serve you. If you want, you can then go back to earlier chapters and work on other tools.

In this chapter, we're going to discuss important topics (like changing our thinking!), and then I offer a set of exercises that will hopefully open your mind to the possibilities before you.

Laying the Foundation

By setting an intention and having some ideas about where you want to go, you can create a vision for the future you desire. You don't have to feel "stuck" or unhappy because you don't know what to do. Rest assured that, in the words of the great literary figure Goethe, when we are bold, great forces will support us.

It's easier to be bold when you have confidence in your vision. For me, confidence comes from feeling prepared, in spite of the uncertainty. If you have worked through previous chapters on skills, strengths, and values, you have a solid foundation for creating your vision of meaningful work. You have considered yourself from different perspectives and hopefully can bring these new realizations to your search.

Whether you have completed all the exercises in previous chapters or not, I hope you consider one or two tools from this book as levers to pull to help you get out of the rut of thinking "the same way" about work and what you want to do. The reason I wrote this book is to share as many tools and ideas as possible to help you find your way. Maybe it's boss shopping (chapter 11); maybe it's a networking tip (chapter 8) or something you learned from one of the case studies (listed in the table of contents, each speaks to the topic of its chapter). Perhaps when you discuss things with a friend, a whole new idea will pop into your head. I hope at least one of the tools in this book leads you somewhere new. Try some of them and notice what happens—there's no right or wrong way to do any of them!

And then, try at least two of the following:

1. **Realistically examine and write down your strengths, weaknesses, skills, and values.** I encourage you to spend at least a few hours thinking about this topic in whatever way works for you. Maybe that just means talking it over with a friend; maybe you decide to ask someone to mentor you through this part of the process (check out chapter 9 for advice on successfully working with a mentor). I hope you'll decide that your future is worth the energy this will take. Write down your thoughts and ideas no matter what process you follow. When I read through my old writing, I realize how far I've come and how one thing I did lead to another, which helped lead to another.

2. **Learn to give to get.** If this isn't intuitive for you, I strongly encourage you to build this into your thinking and how you relate to others. If we recognize ourselves as personally powerful, just by the very fact that we are born and walk the earth, then by extension, I hope you'll perceive others this way too. That doesn't mean we should just trust everyone and anyone at any time. I'm a big believer in *trust but verify.* That said, I hope you will understand that selfishly asking people to help you, without thinking about what's in it for them, is self-defeating. There are thousands of ways to give without expecting anything in return. The benefits are plentiful. Each of us has talents, skills, and energy that might benefit others. Understand those which you can give without draining yourself and you will have a very valuable tool.

3. **Change jobs.** Many millennials and Gen Zers jump from job to job and don't think anything about it. Sometimes jumping from one job to another is a sign of energy, and sometimes it's a sign of laziness. Of course, don't stay in a dead-end job just for the sake of not switching. But if you leave a job because you are bored, it may be useful to think about your own attitude toward the job. Jumping to the next thing may work out great, or maybe you'll just repeat a pattern. While you may be gaining experience with each change, you also may be leaving the impression with future employers that you can't put your head down and accept responsibility for your choices.

4. **Develop a growth mindset.**[26] Personal and career growth relate to:

   - ❦ Being a lifelong learner
   - ❦ Sustaining ourselves in down times
   - ❦ Seeing "failure" as useful and inevitable
   - ❦ Taking reasonable risks
   - ❦ Seeking out and accepting criticism
   - ❦ Accepting responsibility for our future

When we know ourselves as capable of learning, growing, and changing, we are better prepared to face an uncertain future.

Embrace Your Unique Self

The key takeaway I want you to have—not just from this chapter but from the entire book—is that you are unique and special. Throughout your life's journey—both in your career and outside it—there will be people who will try to tear you down. We talked in chapter 2 about messages of "unbelonging" you may have received along the way. Hopefully you've done some of the exercises in that chapter to relieve yourself of that burden. If not, please take time to fully embrace this belief:

You are like no one else. If you are someone who has felt "less than," gather resources around you to support a positive idea of your special identity and talents. I know you are amazing, not because of what you do but because of who you are. This doesn't mean you get special treatment; it means that you deserve the opportunity to try things that are or may be different from what others tell you to do.

Our sense of purpose and pride can be porous, subject to the whims of people in perceived and real power. If we are dependent on these individuals for our livelihood, our choices become limited. Have you ever taken a class, a job, a meeting because someone else thought it would be a good idea? Especially if something inside you told you not to? When we betray ourselves in this way, we suffer. However difficult it is to say no, we benefit from learning to do so.

Once you stand strong in who you are, you are on your way to creating a solid foundation for moving closer to work that feeds you.

Turn Off the Critical Voices

As you go through some of the exercises in this book, you may hear an internal voice of negative self-talk. As I moved throughout my life and career, I had so many voices in my head telling me that I couldn't or shouldn't do something. Here are some sources of negative talk that maybe you have struggled with too.

Parents: My parents were most worried about financial stability. I thought that if I didn't work for that stability, something terrible would happen to me. Maybe you've received similar advice. The problem is that what is relevant to one generation, may not be relevant to another.

Most of you will have ten to twenty jobs in your career. There likely won't be long-term stability in your work life. You will need to adapt over and over again to keep earning a living. Trying to find "meaningful" work in the midst of all that will be even more challenging. You can do it but managing the expectations and worries of loved ones while you follow your process, whatever that is, will be challenging. If you can, thank them for their love and support and then do what you must. Obviously, this becomes trickier when someone else is paying your way. It's their money, and they get to decide how to spend it. The sooner you can become independent financially, the easier it will be to be grateful for their support but not let their voices derail you.

Popular opinion: Finding meaningful work is not about getting a "good" job, although you might get lucky and find work that is meaningful to you that pays well. The search is about finding ways to spend your productive and money-earning time and talents. Invest in understanding yourself and what you want, and you have a fighting chance at getting it.

Except when the country is in a serious recession, finding a job is generally not that difficult, as you probably already know. But finding work that you enjoy and admire is a whole different ballgame. To be a successful baseball player (I love baseball), there are a broad set of skills required, but equally important is mental preparation, stamina (162 games a year), teamwork, and practice. I doubt there's a successful baseball player who would say that skill alone made them a happy or fulfilled player. The question is, what skills (physical, psychological, and emotional) make a good player, and which of those do you have that you could use to help you find work you love?

To have meaningful work, I had to find a way to turn those well-intended voices off. I had to find a way to envision what I wanted and then go and get it. What kept me going was turning off any voice that limited me or suggested that my path should be a certain way. I ignored those voices. I hope you will too.

Go ahead—picture the possibilities!

Here are some ways to start envisioning your future work.

- ❦ **Vision board:** If you like visuals, gather some magazines or other image sources that speak to you. Cut out phrases, pictures, and anything else that seems right. I recommend you don't think too hard about how you design your board, but I do suggest you wait until you have a bunch of items and have moved them around some. My experience is that some words and pictures "feel" better next to each other. Don't try to make sense of what you're putting on the paper—just do it. The more you try to make it "pretty" or nice or appealing, the further away you are from letting your subconscious tell the story.

    Takeaway: You have a picture of your heart's desire that your mind may not yet "see."

- ❦ **Letter:** Write a letter to your younger, current, or future self. It doesn't matter which. Just do what feels right. In the letter, tell yourself what you've done well in your life, what you hope to improve, and how, in the future, you'd like to spend your time. It doesn't have to be about work. What are the activities that you can't stop doing once you start? What are you engaged in when you lose yourself? There are no rules about how to craft this letter. Do not worry about spelling or grammar—they don't matter. Try to get one page out in a sitting.

    Takeaway: You will finish with a creative, stream-of-consciousness representation of what you value and where you want to go.

- ❦ **Mind map:** A mind map is another approach to letting your subconscious lead the way. If you're unfamiliar with this process, it is a diagram to visually organize information. One idea is to put yourself in the middle (hub) and then create spokes based on whatever makes sense to you. It can show skills and strengths you already have or ones that you want to gain. You could put the job you think you want in the middle and then surround the job with whatever comes to mind. Use your imagination. There are no rules.

Takeaway: Mind maps are valuable for making connections between ideas, events, and concepts in a way that our conscious mind can't. And it's fun.

☙ **Stupid resume:** This is a resume that is the opposite of a real resume. Include all the mistakes that you've made. Ignore the chronology—it's irrelevant. This is supposed to be fun and funny. I, for instance, would include the time I got fired from selling shoes because I wouldn't drag customers over to sell them a purse to match their shoes. Keep it light. Structure it however you want—this is for you.

Takeaway: We learn more when we're having fun. Imagine if an employer asked us to write a resume of our mistakes! You might notice something in this resume that teaches you something important about yourself.

☙ **Invented job position:** Research and keep a list of job titles that you find intriguing. Have fun with it—this doesn't have to be a real position (for example, Crayon Evangelist—Oversees all of the company's graphic design; Project Meanie—Keeps coworkers on schedule). You may discover your unique niche! Here are some more examples:

  ☙ Chief Troublemaker
  ☙ Amazement Officer
  ☙ Digital Prophet
  ☙ VP of Miscellaneous Stuff

Takeaway: Like the stupid resume, dreaming up the job title you would like to have is fun and fruitful. Who knows? Maybe one day you'll invent that job!

☙ **List of the things you loved to do when you were a kid:** Often the seeds of what we love to do are born in our childhood. Your love of frogs or drawing or dancing may seem far away from anything you might do as an adult. But, hey, you never know. Even if it doesn't inform your work life, it may help reignite a passion for a hobby.

Takeaway: Do yourself a favor and try this one.

☙ **Job title and descriptions as pleasure reading:** It's fun to peruse job descriptions. You may be surprised at the places that might be great to work at that you never even considered. How does being the Chief Robot Whisperer sound? What about the Director of First Impressions? Keep a file of the titles and descriptions that delight you. Who knows, maybe you'll get a chance to have or create one of these jobs for yourself one day.

Takeaway: Not only is this fun and uplifting, it's great for making conversation and brainstorming. If you notice a job posted with these creative titles, you might learn something about the company culture too.

🍃 **Traditional plan:** Write a more traditional plan. For those of you who want a more structured approach to this step...

a. **Write down the job position you aspire to have.** It doesn't matter if you can see a clear path to getting there or if your mind is telling you that you can never do or get that job. Don't pay attention. Just keep going.

b. **Research companies that interest you.** Think about all the kinds of places you might like to work. For this exercise, don't think about whether the organization has a job opening, a job that you are qualified for, or what the pay might be. The point of this is to open your mind to interesting places. Include nonprofits, government agencies, museums, factories, anywhere that sounds fun or enriching. While you are making this list, think about people you can connect with who work in places like these. Make a list of questions to ask them about the culture of the organization, the kind of work they do, what they like and don't like. Don't feel the need to share this research with friends or family—it's just for you (but you may find that you want to share!).

c. **Document what you think the requirements are to get this type of work.** Don't stop considering the work because you think it requires a PhD or some other far-fetched requirement to get there. The idea is not to stop yourself before you get started. Just keep writing until you make discoveries about yourself.

d. **List your current skills that seem even somewhat related to this job position.** Be sure to include intangibles like passion for the work, the people, the outcome, whatever you think or feel belongs here.

e. **List the kinds of training, courses, people, resources, information, etc., you might need to move in the direction of this work.** If the job is a stretch from your current experience, don't be discouraged. This is not a list of "have-tos" or "must-dos"—it's a way of thinking about how and where you might spend your time and energy in order to move closer to your goal.

Takeaway: You may be surprised at what you learn about yourself, about cool places to work, and about your future.

Most of the work I did in this area didn't help me in the short term (six to nine months). But when I looked at my version of the letter, vision board, mind map, and others from this list of activities a year or two later, I could see the seeds of my future had been there all along—and that made me trust the process of making a plan in whatever way worked for me.

The steps I took, without thinking about them too much, led to the person, the speech, the class, or the experience that led me to my next gig. If I hadn't taken the time to consider myself and the things that made me uniquely me, I would never have had the opportunities that came my way. The thinking, the writing, the brainstorming, the letters, the letting go...made all the difference.

I believe that both of your generations will lead a revolution in finding meaningful work. It's a revolution because it's likely you will toss out the rule book of previous generations (including eventually, perhaps, this guidebook) and do it your way. It will take a combination of humility and boldness to be part of that revolution.

In 2020, we face immense global changes; buckle up. The road may be bumpy, but please, do not despair. Don't lose faith. Many of life's rewards come from the challenges we face. We will get through this together. I believe in you.

APPENDIX

Short List of General Work and Job Search Resources

These are just a few of the resources that I think might be helpful. Not every resource will work for every person. I suggest you think broadly about the kind of information and support you need. One person might need help with interviewing; another may need support for understanding the salary ranges of different jobs. Seek guidance from videos, websites, experts, and books. Ask friends what is working for them. Think about the entire job search process from research to practical tips.

People Whose Work I Like and Trust

Brené Brown (brenebrown.com)
Amy Cuddy (amycuddy.com)
Seth Godin (sethgodin.com)

Websites with Job Leads, Networks, and Other Career Resources

CareerBuilder (careerbuilder.com)
ZipRecruiter (ziprecruiter.com)
Career Sherpa (careersherpa.net)
Find a Job (usa.gov/find-a-job)
LinkedIn (linkedin.com)
Indeed (indeed.com)

Books

What Color Is Your Parachute? by Richard Nelson Bolles

Presence: Bringing Your Boldest Self to Your Biggest Challenges, by Amy Cuddy

Job Search Tools

- I like the tools, particularly the checklists, at https://careersherpa .net/resources/job-search-tools/.
- Google for Jobs. Google has created a way to search across

job-hunting sites, such as Indeed, and individual companies, including unique job search criteria, location, and more. "Tips for Using Google for Jobs Searches" is one article that could help you navigate this feature: https://www.thebalancecareers.com /google-for-jobs-4140171.

REFERENCES

1 Paul Graham, "How to Do What You Love," January 2006, http://paulgraham.com/love.html.

2 Melissa De Witte, "Instead of 'Finding Your Passion,' Try Developing It, Stanford Scholars Say," Stanford News Service, June 18, 2018, https://news.stanford.edu/2018/06/18/find-passion-may-bad-advice/.

3 Mark Emmons, "Key Statistics about Millennials in the Workplace," Dynamic Signal, October 9, 2018, https://dynamicsignal.com/2018/10/09/key-statistics-millennials-in-the-workplace/.

4 Michael Johnston, "Visual History of the S&P 500," ETF Database, updated August 26, 2013, https://etfdb.com/history-of-the-s-and-p-500/#1985.

5 "Top 30 Largest US Companies in the S&P 500 Index 2020," Disfold, updated June 14, 2020, https://disfold.com/top-us-companies-sp500/.

6 Abby Jackson, "This Chart Shows How Quickly College Tuition Has Skyrocketed Since 1980," *Business Insider*, July 20, 2015, https://www.businessinsider.com/this-chart-shows-how-quickly-college-tuition-has-skyrocketed-since-a1980-2015-7.

7 Daniel Kurt, "Student Loan Debt: 2019 Statistics and Outlook," *Investopedia*, November 15, 2019, https://www.investopedia.com/student-loan-debt-2019-statistics-and-outlook-4772007.

8 Richard Fry, "Millennials Are the Largest Generation in the U.S. Labor Force," Pew Research Center, April 11, 2018, https://www.pewresearch.org/fact-tank/2018/04/11/millennials-largest-generation-us-labor-force/.

9 Sangeeta Badal, "The Business Benefits of Gender Diversity," Gallup, January 20, 2014, https://www.gallup.com/workplace/236543/business-benefits-gender-diversity.aspx.

10 Elaine Pofeldt, "Full-Time Freelancing Lures More Americans," *Forbes*, October 5, 2019, https://www.forbes.com/sites/elainepofeldt/2019/10/05/full-time-freelancing-lures-more-americans/#2e7e24657259.

11 https://www.youtube.com/user/JennaMarbles

12 I adopt this idea from what Brené Brown says in *Braving the Wilderness: The Quest for*

True Belonging and the Courage to Stand Alone (New York: Random House, 2017).

13 Jenna's story is for her to tell, if and when she chooses. I'm telling the story of our work together from my perspective only.

14 Allana Akhtar and Andy Kiersz, "College Grads Still Earn More than Workers with No University Degree. This Map Shows the States with the Widest Salary Gaps," *Business Insider*, July 15, 2019, https://www.businessinsider.com/how-much-more-college -graduates-earn-than-non-graduates-in-every-state-2019-5.

15 Zack Friedman, "Student Loan Debt Statistics in 2019: A $1.5 Trillion Crisis," *Forbes*, February 25, 2019, https://www.forbes.com/sites/zackfriedman/2019/02/25/student -loan-debt-statistics-2019/#68b6c811133f.

16 Anisa Purbasari Horton, "Could Micro-credentials compete with traditional degrees?" BBC, February 17, 2020, https://www.bbc.com/worklife/article/20200212-could-micro -credentials-compete-with-traditional-degrees?ocid=ww.social.link.email.

17 Laurent Probst and Christian Scharff, "A Strategist's Guide to Upskilling," *Leadership*, July 25, 2019, https://www.strategy-business.com/feature/A-strategists-guide-to -upskilling?gko=0bb8b.

18 Jennifer A. Dixon, "Making It Happen," *Library Journal*, June 9, 2017, https://www .libraryjournal.com/?detailStory=making-it-happen-programming.

19 Carter Coudriet, "The Top 25 Two-Year Trade Schools: Colleges That Can Solve the Skills Gap," *Forbes*, August 16, 2018, https://www.forbes.com/sites/cartercoudriet/2018/08/15 /the-top-25-two-year-trade-schools-colleges-that-can-solve-the-skills -gap/#b22e8b43478c.

20 Milja Milenkovic, "The Future of Employment—30 Telling Gig Economy Statistics," Small Biz Genius, August 20, 2019, https://www.smallbizgenius.net/by-the-numbers /gig-economy-statistics/#gref.

21 Glynnis Purcell, "The Top 7 Management Styles: Which Ones Are Most Effective?" Workzone, August 27, 2019, https://www.workzone.com/blog/management-styles/.

22 Amy Cuddy, "Your Body Language May Shape Who You Are" TEDGlobal, June 2012, https://www.ted.com/talks/amy_cuddy_your_body_language_may_shape_who_you _are?language=en.

23 Paul Spiegelman, "10 Elements of Great Company Culture," *Inc.*, June 6, 2012, https://

www.inc.com/paul-spiegelman/great-company-culture-elements.html.

24 Stephanie Vozza, "These Are the Four Different Work Styles and How to Work with Each," *Fast Company*, May 24, 2018, https://www.fastcompany.com/40571008/these-are-the-4-different-work-styles-and-how-to-work-with-each.

25 These two articles provide more great questions you can tailor to your situation: Alison Davis, "These 15 Questions Will Assess Your Company's Culture—and Help You Decide How to Improve It," *Inc.*, March 19, 2018, https://www.inc.com/alison-davis/these-15-questions-will-assess-your-companys-culture-and-help-you-decide-how-to-improve-it.html; Emily Moore, "12 Questions You Should Ask to Uncover Company Culture," Glassdoor, October 18, 2018, https://www.glassdoor.com/blog/questions-to-uncover-company-culture/.

26 Angelina Zimmerman, "Shift to a Growth Mindset with these 8 Powerful Strategies," *Inc.*, October 16, 2016, https://www.inc.com/angelina-zimmerman/the-8-tremendous-ways-for-developing-a-growth-mindset.html.